LESTER

Lester Piggott rode into sporting history on a blustery September afternoon in 1984. He was already a racing legend with more than 4,000 winners behind him in a career spanning nearly forty years. But there was something extra special about this latest triumph in the Doncaster St Leger on the big bay colt, Commanche Run, because it took Piggott's score of wins in the classics to twenty-eight, one more than the nineteenth-century wizard, Frank Buckle had achieved. It crowned a career richly studded with success yet always laced with controversy.

So who is this man whose name is woven so deeply into the fabric of our lives that he has become almost public property? Sometimes, he appears one-dimensional – colourful, but flat. Famous for being famous. Yet the loyalty he inspires is so overwhelming that he would carry our money if he were riding Muffin the Mule.

Sean Pryor describes the rough rides, the tough rides, the winners that should have lost and the losers that should have won. This is the story of the world's greatest ever jockey.

By Sean Pryor

BILLY BEAUMONT: THE LION OF WINTER
McENROE: SUPERMAN OR SUPERBRAT?

Lester
A Biography

Sean Pryor

SIDGWICK & JACKSON
LONDON

First published in Great Britain in 1985 by
Sidgwick & Jackson Limited

First paperback edition published in
Great Britain in 1986 by Sidgwick & Jackson Limited

Copyright © 1985 by Sean Pryor

British Library C.I.P.

Pryor, Sean
   Lester: a biography.
   1. Piggott, Lester.   2. Jockeys ——
   Great Britain ——Biography
   I. Title
   798.4'3'0924   SF336.P5

   ISBN 0–450–38998–7

Printed in Great Britain by
Cox & Wyman Limited, Reading
for Sidgwick & Jackson Limited
1, Tavistock Chambers, Bloomsbury Way
London WC1A 2SG

For
KATE and LAURA

Contents

Acknowledgements

Lester Piggott has been around us so long now he's become part of the furniture. Everybody has heard of him, most of us bet on him, especially when it comes to the Derby. He carries the hopes and hard cash of millions of once-a-year punters every first week in June, yet the curious thing is that a great proportion of those punters have only a vague notion why. I was amazed when researching this biography to discover how little his loyal supporters actually know about his racing record, or even his life. It is as if backing Lester has become a family tradition handed down from father to son – or perhaps, more accurately, from mother to daughter, because that's where the most potent betting force seems to lie. So I hope this book will fill in that shadowy background, for the general reader as well as the serious student of racing.

So many people have lent me their time and their opinions that to acknowledge them all would be to write a second book, at least as long as the first. I hope therefore, they will be content to recognize their contribution in the narrative, but I would like to acknowledge the special debt I owe to Richard Baerlein of *The Guardian*, whose kindly advice helped me firmly into the starting stalls. There is also Rohan Seecoomar, my researcher, who spent endless hours pouring over cuttings in newspaper libraries, and Val Porter, who slaved over the manuscript. Finally, I owe the greatest debt to my editor, Libby Joy, who kept me going with tact and patience when illness threatened to torpedo the whole project.

1 | *The Thrill of the Chase*

Lester Piggott was bred for racing as surely as the animals he has partnered to victories all over the world. Shake any branch of the family tree and you are sure to dislodge a classic winner: a Cannon, a Rickaby, a Piggott, a Day. . .

The dynasty began with John Day, a rumbustious Wiltshire farmer who bred horses for both work and pleasure. He trained on a modest scale but with a fair degree of success and his sons seemed to share his passion for fast, daring animals. Two became jockeys, another a vet. A fourth son turned his back on both farming and racing and emigrated to Russia, but a fifth, John Day III, became not only a noted trainer and breeder, but the father-in-law of Tom Cannon – one of the great jockeys in racing history.

By the end of the nineteenth century, the family had produced a staggering thirty-two classic race winners on the flat. Then came the Piggott connection. Ernest, son of Cheshire farmer Tom Piggott, married Cannon's only daughter Margaret, and it is here that the Piggott legend takes an upward turn. Literally, in fact, because Ernest's passion was for jumpers, and contemporary accounts make much of his balanced brilliance in a tight finish. He was both bold and fearless, qualities that were swiftly evident in his son, Keith Piggott, Lester's father, who though small was acknowledged as one of the toughest men ever to appear on a racecourse.

The final, decisive link in the genealogical chain came when Keith married Iris Rickaby, whose great-grandfather had trained the 1855 Derby winner Wild Dayrell. Their son Lester inherited all the skill, courage and, above all, determination of two generations of outstanding horsemen, and it came to flower at the precociously young age of twelve.

Lester was born on Guy Fawkes Day, 5 November 1935, in the little Berkshire village of Wantage. Lester's association with the village proved fleeting because the family moved a few miles east to Lambourn before he was very old, but it was in Wantage that he first learned to ride.

Father Keith had a small yard and by the time Lester was a toddler he was as familiar with the sights and smells of horses and farmyard animals as he was with his own toys. Naturally enough, his parents harboured ambitions for him to go into the 'family business' and it was with a mixture of excitement and trepidation that they awaited his reaction to Brandy, a New Forest pony bought by Keith for £10.

They had agreed that three was as good an age as any to put the youngster up, and Keith was keen, too, that he should find an animal that would challenge its rider as well as comply. New Forest ponies are noted for their spirit and perhaps it was an excess of this characteristic that led to the name. In any case, Brandy proved difficult to break and Keith was thrown several times before he finally got the measure of the animal. Then it was Lester's turn. He was put up gently and the horse and its new partner walked quietly and harmoniously around the small yard as if they had known each other all their lives. Keith and Iris Piggott were proud and excited. Said Lester's father, 'Well, it looks like we've bred a jockey!'

Until the advent of Brandy, Lester's obsession had been with a pair of cats that followed him everywhere he went, but now his attention was elsewhere. It wasn't long before he was being taught the basics of riding and it was clear from his responses that it presented no problems at all. It is rare for children of three to maintain a high level of concentration, but Lester seemed to. Keith noted the sign.

Lester was born with a slightly cleft palate which gave him a mode of speech that has become the most imitated in sport. It was at about this time that Lester's parents became aware that he was also partially deaf. The impediments have been variously blamed for, or credited with, the aloof, detached manner that characterizes Lester's approach to riding racehorses, but he himself attaches no importance to them. Nevertheless, it must have made school difficult, and it was hard for him to make friends.

Lester's affinity with Brandy prospered and soon the pair were scooping up gymkhana ribbons all over Berkshire. By the time he was six, he was beating children twice his age over sharp little courses at horse shows, and when he was seven his father allowed him to walk out with his racehorses on the downs. He soon outgrew Brandy, and Rip and Diana followed as every waking minute was spent riding, riding, riding.

Lester was alone most of the time, but it was not a lonely life. His father was a stern taskmaster when it came to the business of horses, but the home was a warm and loving one. At no stage of his development was Lester pushed beyond his capacity, but he showed a remarkable ability to absorb lessons and advice, so it was small wonder that by the age of twelve his father considered him mature enough to make his racecourse debut.

It took place on 7 April 1948 at Salisbury, the historic cathedral town in the Wiltshire Vale, and it came on a filly trained by his father at Lambourn. The Chase was a good-natured animal, sensible and responsive, with a useful turn of foot in the right conditions. Lester rode her well enough and soon Keith was putting him up at Bath, Worcester and Kempton Park. By now Keith felt he could win with The Chase and Lester, and in August he found exactly the sort of race he was looking for.

The Wigan Lane Selling Handicap at Haydock Park, to be run on 18 August, was a mile race worth £294 to the winner. There were twelve runners and The Chase went to post at 10/1, just the right kind of price for the trainer. Keith knew Lester was in with an excellent chance, especially as the ground had dried after weeks of relentless rain in the north of

England. *The Times* described the two-day meeting opening 'amid uncut wheat and blackening oats, but in pleasant conditions'.

Lester came through his first challenge brilliantly. He held up The Chase while Miss Annabel and Prompt Corner battled for the lead and then, inside the final furlong, slipped the filly cheekily to the front to win by two lengths. 'Most intelligently ridden by young apprentice L. Piggott,' noted *The Times* in its report of the race. The Chase fetched 330 guineas at the subsequent sale and Lester, no doubt, collected an extra helping of ice cream from his proud father. Ice cream had become a passion, one that was to stay with him until his late teens.

Naturally, the press showed special interest in the winner of Haydock Park's 2.15, but if they were expecting a gushing torrent of youthful chatter they were disappointed. The youngster, his eyes shining with excitement, could manage no more than, 'It was terrific. I rode the last five furlongs hard and managed to pull ahead.' Keith added laconically, 'There is no reason why he should not become a good jockey.' And when mother Iris was telephoned for her reaction her response was, 'Don't spoil him. It's not so wonderful. It was only a selling race.'

Admirable though these attempts were to keep Lester's feet firmly on the ground, they cut little ice with the newspapers who now began to chronicle his exploits and search for comparisons with the greats like Steve Donoghue and Gordon Richards. There were the 'human interest' pieces too. The *News Chronicle* under the headline, 'BOY 12 BEAT STAR JOCKEYS' revealed: 'He wants to be a jockey but he is in the middle of his schooldays and he will have to be back with his books at Miss Westlake's private school when the summer is over. Lester spends most of his spare time in the stables. He gets up at 7 a.m. and helps exercise the horses before school. He's been riding since he was three, says his mother, and he is pretty good – though not a patch on his father.'

The debut season ended for Lester with two second places to add to his tally. At 5 stone he was a 'hot thing' for trainers looking for handicap winners and, not surprisingly, his services were much in demand in 1949. He was able to manage 120 rides between terms and with 6 winners, 8 seconds and 39 thirds, he was clearly learning fast. Finally, it was agreed with the local education authorities that the youngster should have private lessons. He was clearly going to be a full-time jockey when he left school at fourteen; still, whenever he had an afternoon off for racing, he had to compensate with extra lessons.

So Lester was getting a solid education as well as the chance to learn his trade. He claimed at the time not to like lessons, but then all schoolchildren do. According to his teachers, he showed a particular aptitude for history, which he enjoyed, and maths. There was one other subject at which he was later to excel, but sadly it was not on Miss Westlake's curriculum – studying form!

2 | Zucchero

The long, dark nights and bitter-bleak mornings must have seemed endless to a young boy dreaming of gaudy silks and the sweet smell of summer grass. But there were horses to be done, tack to be hauled, buckets to be filled. Mucking-out was a chore, grooming a pleasure. It is in these quiet, intimate moments that bonds between horse and rider are forged. And when, finally, the cutting edge of winter surrendered to the softness of spring, Lester Piggott was ready.

The racing world was not.

There was nothing self-effacing about the 1950 version of Fleet Street's newly christened 'Boy Wonder'. The style was all blood and thunder, flailing whip and flashing stirrup. He rode as if the hounds of hell were snapping at his heels. And, in a sense, they were. It wasn't long before Piggott's exploits became the talk of the Jockey Club.

In a modest handicap race at Hurst Park, he forced Sailor's Knot into third place, bumping and boring his way onto the rails. The stewards winced and promptly stood him down for twenty-four hours. It was his first suspension. A second followed in July. This time he was involved in a scrimmage on the filly Trumps Green rounding the final turn in the Moderate Plate. Another twenty-four hours out of the saddle. And one month later, Lester was stood down again, this time by the stewards at Worcester. He was fast becoming a marked man.

But he was also becoming a winner. Victory on Blue Sapphire in the Kent Handicap at Folkestone gave him his twenty-fifth success and moved him up to the status of 3 lb claimer. The apprentice allowance in racing consists of weight reductions according to a boy's rate of progress. Until he has ridden six winners, an apprentice is permitted to carry 7 lb less than the stipulated weight; then 5 lb up to twenty-five winners, 3 lb up to forty winners, and thereafter he meets his elders on equal terms. By early September, Lester was nudging that magical mark.

The press were by now tracking his every move. It is highly unusual for a jockey to come out of his apprenticeship so early. The late Frank Wootton managed it at the age of thirteen, just before the First World War, but he was in every way an exception. (At fifteen he was champion jockey with 165 winners and before his eighteenth birthday he had carried off the title four times.) By contrast, such legends of the turf as Sir Gordon Richards and Steve Donoghue were late to shed their allowance. Richards was nineteen, Donoghue twenty-one.

On 20 September, Lester was booked to partner the filly Zina in the Brighton Autumn Cup over the switchback sea-side course. Opposing him that day would be his idol, the peerless Gordon Richards, whose mount Sporting Offer had twice won over the course and distance and was a warm favourite. Lester rode the most mature race of his young life, flashing past the winning post five lengths clear of his rivals with the champion jockey way down the field. He had come of age.

In the *Daily Mail*, Captain Heath summed up the scale of his achievement: 'The boy, now on equal terms with senior jockeys before his 15th birthday, will not lack rides as a consequence because he combines judgement with vigour and courage. His achievement yesterday quite overshadowed the three successes of Gordon Richards, who in each case was at his brilliant best.'

Said the youngster: 'I expected to do it at Leicester on Tuesday when my grandfather came to see me ride for the first time. I may be riding as a freelance next year.'

So impressed were Zina's connections with his handling of

the big filly that they rewarded him with the ride in the season's final major handicap, the Cambridgeshire at Newmarket. Zina's Brighton win would have earned the filly a 9 lb
penalty had the race been worth £1,000, or more. In fact it
fell short of that figure by exactly £7 7s. 0d. so Piggott would
only have to carry an extra 3 lb – which made Zina a very
lively candidate indeed.

After Brighton, the winners began to come thick and fast
and by October he had topped the half-century. Then at
Newbury, on the Friday before the Cambridgeshire, disaster
struck.

A visiting Australian jockey objected to Piggott's handling
of Barnacle in the Manton Handicap, claiming that the colt
had bumped and bored his mount Royal Oak IV so badly
that he was prevented from winning. The local stewards sustained the objection and Barnacle was placed last. Piggott
was ordered to appear before the Jockey Club stewards at
Newmarket on the morning of the big race.

The visiting Australian was Arthur Edward (Scobie)
Breasley. It was the first crossing of swords by the two men
who would thrill racegoers throughout the late fifties and
early sixties.

It is ironical to reflect on that first encounter. Breasley's
experience of stewards and discipline in his apprentice days
in Sydney in the 1930s almost exactly paralleled Piggott's. In
his official biography, *A Lifetime in Racing*, written by Christopher Poole, Breasley is quoted as saying:

It seemed that I was called in – and stood down – for the
same things that other riders were doing and getting away
with. When you're young and fearless you try tactics you
would not attempt in later life, but you have to have a little
devil in order to succeed. Perhaps some of the strokes I pulled
did put other jockeys in danger but I don't think I was any
worse than the rest.

Next day, Piggott was back in action in the Reading
Stakes, a ten-furlong handicap, and his partner was again
Zina. Despite putting up almost two stone of dead weight,

Piggott coaxed the filly to a half-length victory over Happy Haven ridden by his cousin, Bill Rickaby. It was a brilliant performance. Zina was barely blowing at the end and was clearly going to be super-fit for the big race. Lester's on-course manners had been so impeccable that racegoers found it hard to believe that this was the same jockey they had watched the day before.

The boy's first appearance in racing's 'Star Chamber', the Newmarket headquarters of the Jockey Club, came at ten o'clock on the morning of the Cambridgeshire. The shy four-teen-year-old found himself facing the Earl of Sefton, Lord Irwin and Major R. Macdonald Buchanan. The interview was painfully brief. He was told that notice of his reckless rid-ing throughout the summer had been duly taken and it was decided to suspend him from racing for the rest of the season.

On the face of it, the ban was severe. But the season's end was less than a month away and the stewards, clearly out to make a point rather than exact retribution, granted him a day's dispensation so that he could accept two rides that afternoon and, most important of all, partner Zina in the Cambridgeshire.

At nine furlongs straight, the Cambridgeshire often resembles something of a cavalry charge. It certainly did on this day, and leading the thirty-one runners in a dash for the truest ground on the stand rails was Lester Piggott. Coming out of Newmarket's famous Dip, Piggott felt sure his group held the advantage over the runners on the other side of the course. He stung Zina into one last flourish and they flashed past the winning post with Valdesco close up.

So sure was the youngster that he had snatched the sea-son's last big prize that he had no hesitation in nudging his mount into the winner's enclosure.

'We did it by half a length,' he told his father.

Others were less convinced. The judge called for a photo-graph and after a few minutes the result was announced. 'First Kelling, second Zina, third Valdesco. The distances, a neck and half a length.' Lester was stunned, but the evidence was irrefutable. In that last headlong dash for the line, Lester had failed to notice the fast-finishing Kelling with the acknowledged master of Newmarket, Doug Smith, riding for his life.

Later he reflected on the decision: 'I thought I had won. Zina had to race by herself. Had there been something alongside us I think she would have pulled out more. When I was going down the straight I thought the race was in my pocket.' But there were no youthful tears, no bitterness, no recriminations. Now it was back to Lambourn and racing wilderness.

Next morning, the *Daily Mail* carried a picture of the youngster back at his lessons. The story read:

> The hands of Lester Piggott, which guided 52 horses to victory this season, busied themselves with arithmetic books yesterday. For Lester, described by experts as the boy who could be in the £12,000 a year jockey class next year, was back in school. And until next March, when his suspension from racing ends, there he will be every day. Surprisingly, Lester does not mind school one bit. Said Mrs Jessie Paul who teaches him in Lambourn, Berkshire, 'He really wants to learn.' Said Lester at home last night, 'I'm really looking forward to next season.'

Still, there was plenty to console him as he sat at his desk. Those 52 winners, which had made him Champion Apprentice for the first time, had come from 404 rides with 45 seconds and 39 thirds. In the frame 136 times, an average strike of one place every 2.97 rides. That was the kind of arithmetic Lester appreciated most!

The racing press continued to run articles about the Wonder Boy. Even when he was out of the saddle, he was rarely out of the news. H. de Winton Wigley analyzed his progress in relation to other outstanding apprentices in an article in the *News Chronicle*:

> He has not set a record by coming out of his apprenticeship so early. Yet Lester is plainly on the track of the masters. Herbert Jones, as an apprentice, won the Triple Crown [2,000 Guineas, Derby, St Leger] in 1900 riding Diamond Jubilee for the Prince of Wales. The year he finished his apprenticeship, Charlie Elliott was at the head of the jockeys' list.

He also won the 2,000 Guineas as an apprentice. But in the hands of Lester Piggott, aged 14, is a great future – as great, possibly, as the past of Steve Donoghue and the present of Gordon Richards.

The *Daily Express* interviewed Lester's mother on the youngster's fifteenth birthday. There had been no games, no other children to help blow out the candles on his cake. Explained Iris Piggott: 'We wanted him to have a party but Lester lives in his world and only seems to come alive at race meetings.' Keith, meanwhile, found himself fielding questions about his son's aggressive riding style. 'Lester was only going for gaps that he was entitled to go for. He wasn't using rough riding tactics. Everybody started to pick on him.' As always, Lester kept his own counsel.

The next year, 1951, was Festival of Britain Year. It was a year which in racing was to see the emergence of the Irish as a serious force in the classics equation, the institution of a £30,000 race for the first time – the King George VI and Queen Elizabeth Stakes – and a series of doping scandals which were to rock the establishment to its foundations.

The growth in popularity of ante-post betting on the major races had spawned a sinister cottage industry – fixing races. Security, even at the big stables, was frequently lax and with less sophisticated techniques of chemical analysis than we know today, it was sometimes hard to detect when a horse had been 'got at'. The stewards of the Jockey Club became edgy as the press allegations mounted, and finally they panicked, producing a piece of legislation that was to have a profound (and disastrous) effect for years to come.

In an amendment to rule 102 (on doping) a paragraph was added stating: 'If in any case it shall be found that any drug or stimulant has been administered to a horse for the purpose of affecting its speed in a race, the licence of the trainer of the horse shall be withdrawn and he shall be declared a disqualified person.'

Just how sharp and indiscriminate the teeth of this legal crocodile were to become was revealed in December of that year when Lord Rosebery, one of the pillars of the racing establishment, offered a reward of £1,000, via a letter to the Press Association, for information leading to the conviction of those responsible for doping his horse Snap. Snap, trained at Newmarket by Jack Jarvis, had started 5/2 favourite for the Dalham Stakes at Newmarket on 31 October and finished a miserable twelfth.

The stewards did not order an official test, but Lord Rosebery had one conducted privately. It proved positive, as he later revealed. The point was that, had the test been official, Jarvis would have lost his licence, without appeal, despite the fact that he was a completely innocent party. Later, Vincent O'Brien, the most successful trainer in the history of flat racing, was to fall innocently foul of that pernicious paragraph in rule 102.

The doping scandals would continue for many years, and Lester Piggott and Noel Murless, the trainer with whom he dominated the classics between 1955 and 1966, were to become victims in the most celebrated case of all.

But that was far into the future. At the dawn of 1951, while Britain prepared to celebrate a reprieve from the years of post-war austerity, Lester Piggott was preparing his own celebration – the day he could once more pull on the silks and ride out for victory on a thoroughbred racehorse.

He didn't have to wait long.

Lester began 1951 as he had ended 1950 – a winner. The victories toppled one upon another as he set a ferocious pace in pursuit of a second apprentice jockey's title. His greatest success would come with the 100/8 shot Mystery IX in the prestigious Eclipse Stakes at Sandown, and he would make the acquaintance, too, of one of the most remarkable horses in turf history, the wily, wilful Zucchero. As James Lawton has noted tellingly in an earlier biography of the maestro, 'The fact is that Zucchero was to be to the shaping of Lester Piggott what the first battle is to a trained fighting man. After it he knows he is so much stronger. He knows what he can do. He has proved something to himself.'

Zucchero was a pig. A horse that could (Lawton again), 'leave a trainer suspended between heaven and hell'. He stood sixteen hands and could move as sweetly over the turf as a skimming swallow. When he was in the mood. But for Zucchero, that wasn't often. He was the despair of his first trainer, Ken Cundell, who knew the animal possessed a god-given gift but had neither the time nor, ultimately, the patience to mine the hidden gold. Lester Piggott was given the ride in the 1951 Derby. If anyone could make contact with Zucchero, it would be him.

He was given little chance to find out. Zucchero went to the start calmly enough, but as the tapes went up he swung round and was left for dead as the field galloped off up the hill. Ironically, it was one of the poorest fields in Derby history and had the animal not turned moody at the last minute, who knows what might have happened. The race was won by Arctic Prince by six lengths from Sybil's Nephew with Signal Box, ridden by the great Irish steeplechase jockey, Martin Molony, third. The winning rider, Charlie Spares, summed up his victory with a remark that has gone down in racing folklore. 'The others must be awful, guvnor, as ours ain't much!'

Cundell let Zucchero go, with reluctance, but also, one suspects, with a sense of relief. Another trainer, Bill Payne, was given the task of finding his true worth and he too turned to Piggott to do the searching. They came together again for the inaugural running of the King George VI and Queen Elizabeth Stakes and Piggott rode him brilliantly to take a valuable second place. Contact had been made. Such was the transformation in the animal that he was actually quoted as favourite for the Doncaster St Leger, but meanwhile Piggott again had the ride in the Oxfordshire Stakes at Newbury in August.

It was an interesting race, not least because it confirmed Zucchero's growing stature, but also because it matched for the first time the King and the Pretender to his throne in a match-race where tactics are everything. Gordon Richards was the king and his mount, Le Sage, was probably not half as talented as Zucchero. But, with Richards to guide him, Le Sage proved a very handy winner. Lester was disappointed, but the defeat taught him many valuable lessons, lessons that would be rammed down the throat of many another jockey in years to come. Captain Heath summed up the encounter in the *News Chronicle* this way:

> In a match, tactics play the most important part, and in this case, Zucchero's opponent, Le Sage, was ridden by that master tactician, Gordon Richards, whereas Zucchero was in the hands of the brilliant but still comparatively inexperienced Lester Piggott. Granted that Piggott may have had riding orders and doubtless tried to carry them out, what chance could he have in a contest of brains with The Master?

It was the last time anyone would write that about him.

In the event, Zucchero did not win the Leger, but there were triumphs awaiting him still and Piggott would share them. Meanwhile, their partnership was temporarily dissolved when Lester suffered a crashing fall on 25 August at Lingfield Park after Eph Smith's horse had thrown his rider, fifty yards from the winning post. In the ensuing mêlée, several horses and riders went to ground. Lester broke his collar bone but, more seriously, he also broke two bones in his left leg. Once again, a brilliant season had come prematurely to an end.

But so far ahead of his contemporaries was the youngster from Lambourn that at the end of the season the apprentice jockeys' table again read: First: Lester Piggott. This time, his winning haul was fifty-one and had fate not taken such a decisive intervention it would surely have been many more.

3
Gay Time

Lester was undoubtedly a more mature rider in 1951. He continued to give jockeys nightmares and stewards palpitations with his dashing style, but the brushes with authority were fewer. He was already building up a reputation as a tactical rider and a patient one. He had also shown physical courage. Soon, he would add strength to his formidable armoury of talents and then he would be complete.

But it was the journey from boyhood to manhood that raised the only serious question about his future. Lester was growing. Fast. He was already as tall as former champion jockey Harry Wragg, at 5 ft 8 in one of the tallest men ever to make a success on the flat. In August, John Rickman summed up the growing doubts in a thoughtful article in the *Daily Mail*. Under the headline, 'THE GROWING WONDER BOY', he wrote:

> Will 15-year-old Lester Piggott, the Wonder Boy, be champion before he is 21 (in 1957)? This is the question that the racing world has been asking since this gifted lad made it plain last year that he was a starlet of the saddle. If he continues to grow and put on weight as he has done in the past three years the answer is: possible but improbable.
>
> It should be understood that for a jockey to have a reasonable chance of being champion on the flat his riding weight must not be in excess of 8 st. 7 lb. The reason is obvious: there are not too many rides to be had at 9 st. or over, but there are unlimited opportunities for the jockey who can ride at

around 8 st., as Gordon Richards has done for many years.

Bearing this in mind, consider these figures (his birthday is November 5):

Age	Date	Weight
12	March 1948	4 st. 11 lb or 67 lb
13	March 1949	5 st. 6 lb or 76 lb
14	March 1950	6 st. 0 lb or 84 lb
15	March 1951	6 st. 9 lb or 93 lb
15	August 1951	7 st. 1 lb or 99 lb
16	March 1952	7 st. 4 lb or 102 lb ?
17	March 1953	7 st. 13 lb or 111 lb ?
18	March 1954	8 st. 8 lb or 120 lb ?

It will be seen that from March 1948 to March 1951 his weight has increased about 9 lb a year. If he continues to grow at that rate, he will be 8 st 8 lb in the spring of 1954 at the age of 18½, and over 9 st. the next year.

There is no knowing what Nature will do. Lester might stop growing and putting on weight tomorrow, but seeing that he is a normal, healthy boy who keeps very fit, this is unlikely, particularly as his parents realize it would be asking for trouble in years to come if weight control were seriously and consistently attempted.

Reading that must have given Lester a jolt. It was the first ominous hint of the agonies that might lie ahead if his ambition was to be champion of the Flat. At fifteen, he showed a healthy appetite for ice cream. He still does. But few who knew the youngster or his father doubted that, when the time came to make the sacrifices, he would be equal to them.

Because of his outstanding natural ability, an alternative career under National Hunt Rules was an obvious possibility. Rickman suggested as much.

If he does continue to grow he may be another Martin Molony, who at a riding weight of approximately 9 st. can hold his best with the champions of both codes – Flat and National Hunt. And if it comes to National Hunt and the rough and tumble of steeplechasing and hurdling, Lester should make a great name for himself, for his father met with considerable success at this game and has already passed on a number of hints to his boy.

But, for now, hurdling was a hobby, flat racing a career.

And that career seemed about to take a decisive turn when it was announced in February 1952 that Lester was to be first jockey to Mrs J. V. Rank, whose horses were trained by Noel Cannon at Druids Lodge, while remaining apprenticed to his father at Lambourn. Scobie Breasley had been offered the position, but after being so used to the sun on his back, he had become disenchanted with the English climate and shipped himself back to Australia. His departure had left Cannon in something of a dilemma. Mrs Rank had inherited the string following the sudden death of her husband in January and it seemed more than possible that she would sell out her racing interests altogether. Cannon turned to his cousin Keith Piggott for help and they quickly agreed that Lester should sign on. It was the first contract he ever signed.

Because of his broken leg, Lester's activities in the yard at Lambourn had been restricted. Even after the plaster had been removed, he had still found trouble bending his knee and it took plenty of hard, painful exercise to rebuild the wasted muscle. 'It was agony,' he said. 'I found it very difficult to bend my knee again. I kept having to grab hold of my ankle and pull the leg up under me to make the knee bend. But after a while it did begin to loosen up and finally it was as good as ever.'

But the forced inactivity had also taken a more serious toll. When he emerged in March 1952 to begin the new season, his weight had leaped to 7 st. 12 lb – over half a stone more than the gloomy prediction John Rickman had made for him. It seemed Piggott's prime racing time was now, or else it might be never.

Noel Cannon held a modest hand at Druids Lodge, but tucked in there was a possible ace – Gay Time, a colt out of Daring Miss and a full brother to the useful Elopement. As a two-year-old, the big chestnut had shown real promise in winning the Richmond Stakes at Goodwood and the Solario Stakes at Sandown Park. He was immediately aimed at the 2,000 Guineas.

The going was good at Newmarket and should have suited Gay Time, but he ran poorly and finished unplaced. Cannon concluded that he needed longer to come to hand and began a training programme aimed at the Derby in June. The horse that was to figure so prominently in Gay Time's life, Tulyar, would also be at Epsom and would go to the post a warm favourite.

Lester had his first ride on the colt in a minor race at Salisbury in May. Gay Time showed good speed to win easily, but the opposition was moderate and there was barely a ripple in the market. Tulyar, on the other hand, caused a genuine surge of excitement by his victory in the Derby trial at Lingfield Park. He had not proved difficult to train – his temperament was notably placid – but he had proved hard to assess. Trainer Marcus Marsh felt sure he would be unsuited to hard ground and in that dry, hot spring and early summer the going was not in his favour.

Marsh had bypassed the 2,000 Guineas, to the chagrin of the Aga Khan's son, Prince Aly, who now controlled the ageing owner's interests, and as Derby Day approached, with still no give in the ground, Marsh became increasingly worried for his colt's chances at Epsom. Five days before the race, Tulyar was given a stiff, five-furlong work-out. Charlie Smirke, his jockey, was supposed to bring him up a peat moss strip but, instead, galloped the colt along a parallel track which racing historian Roger Mortimer described as 'as hard as the Cromwell Road'. Marsh was reportedly furious when Tulyar pulled up, but Smirke calmly informed him that the horse acted even better on the top of the ground.

News of the successful work-out must have leaked out because the Derby course proved as unyielding as predicted when the big day dawned. Yet Tulyar was heavily backed in the market, down from 100/8 to 11/2 favourite. Lester Piggott and Gay Time were 25/1.

The race was to mark another watershed in Lester's young life. He found himself embroiled in one of the roughest, toughest Derbies in recent memory. He received a fearful battering on the swing through Tattenham Corner, and when Tulyar took it up two furlongs from home, Lester found himself with an acre of ground to make up.

But Gay Time kept on improving until, with just 100 yards to go, he was sniffing at Tulyar's flying heels. As they came out of the dip and up the hill, Lester's mount was fast running out of fuel and, as tired horses will often do, began to hang to the left. Smirke was able to keep Tulyar going just that fraction better and they passed the winning post three parts of a length to the good. 'What did I Tulyar?' yelled the irrepressible jockey as he rode the Derby winner into the winner's enclosure.

It was a bitterly disappointing moment for the youngster who was aiming to become the youngest ever Derby winner in recorded history. But there was worse to come. As they passed the post, Gay Time slipped forward onto his nose and Lester went cartwheeling to the turf. The frightened colt righted itself and promptly bolted, leaving a bruised and bemused jockey to wander forlornly back to the jockeys' changing room, unable to weigh in.

It was fully twenty minutes before Gay Time was arrested by a mounted policeman and ridden back to the unsaddling enclosure by a stable lad. By then, Piggott was already changed into his silks for the next race. But despite the incident, Gay Time's saddle cloth had remained intact and Lester was able to go to the scales and be officially declared second. As he sat glumly on the scales, he reflected bitterly on the race. It had been a nightmare and he was convinced that he had been cheated of victory by Tulyar leaning on him in the final 100 yards. He told trainer Noel Cannon he wanted to object.

Mrs Rank would not hear of it, and neither would Cannon. Both believed Piggott was over-reacting to the disappointment of coming so close to the ultimate prize and then suffering the added indignity of being unseated. But there were many sage observers at Epsom that day who were convinced that Piggott was right. Had an objection been sustained, Gay Time would have been the first horse to win the Derby on a disqualification since Aboyeur was adjudged to have been jostled by Graganour on the run-in in 1913.

Still Lester would not be consoled. He felt sure he had been cheated. But he was given a swift chance to avenge the defeat at Royal Ascot in the rich King George VI and Queen Elizabeth Stakes. This time there was no interference, supposed or otherwise, but still it was Tulyar that got the verdict – this time by just a neck.

In retrospect, one could argue that Lester and Gay Time

were an unlucky combination, but Tulyar was to prove himself a worthy champion and carry off the St Leger later in the year after Gay Time moved stables, first to Walter Nightgall at Epsom and then to Noel Murless at Beckhampton. He was probably an unlucky horse, and he proved a disappointing stallion too, after being purchased for a then record price of £50,000 to stand at the National Stud.

Gay Time did win once more as a three-year-old, in the Gordon Stakes at Goodwood with Gordon Richards aboard, but in Tulyar's St Leger he made no worthwhile show at all. Funnily enough, he almost exacted some sort of oblique revenge in that race. Gordon Richards remembers: 'He ran well for one and a quarter miles, but then there was nothing left. Smirke on Tulyar nearly got into trouble over this, he was trailing me, naturally thinking that, as an old rival, Gay Time was the danger. But he saw in a flash that I was done. He got out just in time to win.'

Years later, Lester Piggott would tell the late Jack Wood of the *News of the World* in one of his most revealing interviews:

I shall never forgive myself for losing that Derby. Smirke won the race on Tulyar and he kidded everyone that he won easily. But had I not been so young, had not so many things gone wrong, Charlie would never have made his famous 'What did I Tulyar?' remark as he dismounted.

Charlie was a bit of a showman, but a greater rider. Although I had ridden my first winner four years earlier, I was still a kid and after Gay Time had lost a shoe, I felt oddly nervous as I went down to the start after all the others. We did not get away as we should have done and my horse did not have enough pace to keep up with the leaders, which is essential going into Tattenham Corner. I did not give the colt the right sort of race. I was, I suppose, a little raw. The race calls for guts as well as skill. The stretch after the winning post is the most dangerous in the world. The last straw on Gay Time came when he pitched on his nose when we reached the road by the big pub. Maybe it was his way of telling me I had ridden a stinker.

Like any youngster of sixteen, Lester was reluctant to acknowledge defeat and disappointment as parts of the learning process. He tended to treat any setback with defiance in those days, blue eyes flashing angrily at the injustice of it all. He said little, however, even when he was deprived of the ride on his beloved Zucchero in the first running of the Washington International at Laurel in Maryland. Mrs Rank had a runner at Sandown Park on the same day and retaining rights were enforced. Zucchero was eventually just touched off by Wilwyn in a spectacularly fast race but showed just how much he had improved since those wilful early days.

But, overall, the move to Mrs Rank had worked well. Lester's score jumped to seventy-nine and he finished fifth in the jockeys' table. He had earned for Mrs Rank and other owners a handsome £23,390 in prize money and Lester's own season's earnings didn't fall far short of £5,000. As an apprentice, he was entitled to only half that amount. But as his 'Master' continued to be his father, I think it's safe to say it all found its way into Lester's burgeoning account.

The success of Tulyar in repulsing the French challenge in two of the five major classics made 1952 a memorable year. It could have been even greater – as great even as 1935 when Barham carried off the Triple Crown. At least that was the opinion of Prince Aly Khan, who managed the colt on behalf of his now ailing father. Marcus Marsh's decision not to run Tulyar in the 2,000 Guineas on account of the firm ground still rankled with the young Prince and it was no real surprise when he moved his horses (Tulyar did not stay in training as a four-year-old) to Noel Murless. Murless had won over £22,000 for his owners in 1951, sending out forty-five winners from his Beckhampton yard with the incomparable Gordon Richards aboard. It didn't quite compare with the sixty-four winners that had made him champion trainer in 1948 for the first time, but that was the year of Abernant and Goblet and his first 1,000 Guineas classic winner, Queenpot. With the new Queen confirming that she would continue an association begun by the late King George VI, and other owners equally keen to place their horses, it was clear that Murless in 1952 was getting set to take off. He was also on the move. Murless had finally had enough of Beckhampton and his

major owner, the irascible Mr Arthur Dewar, and bought
the Warren Place stables at Newmarket. It was to be the
start of a dynasty which dominated racing in Britain for over
a decade, and continues to this day via Murless's son-in-law,
Henry Cecil.

Lester began the 1953 season – Coronation season – in fine
style. He was soon among the winners, and at Epsom he was
reunited with Zucchero in the Coronation Cup. The colt had
wintered well and looked very fit and very strong, but his
temperament remained as unpredictable as ever. Somehow,
Lester was able to calm the horse. The French-trained Dyna-
mite was a strong favourite in the race, and Wilwyn, Zucchero's Washington conqueror, was also strong in the market.

The danger point for Zucchero had always been the start
where the milling horses often had an unsettling effect on
him. But not this day. He went down as gently as a lamb, and
when the tapes went up he was away smoothly and without
fuss.

Lester was beginning to get the hang of the tricky Epsom
course by now and he tucked Zucchero in the middle of the
field for the first half-mile, improving to sixth as they
rounded Tattenham Corner. In the straight Lester urged
him on and the colt responded readily. As trainer Bill Payne
put it, 'He began picking them off.' Zucchero came home a
handsome winner with Wilwyn relegated to third place. It
was the biggest moment yet in the youngster's career and the
smile of joy on his face as they entered the unsaddling enclosure told it all.

A few weeks later, Lester pocketed another big prize when
he steered home the 20/1 outsider Absolve in the Queen's
Vase at Royal Ascot. The two-mile race calls for a strong
horse and a thinking jockey. Lester showed just how much
he had come on as a tactician and judge of pace by his performance that day.

But there were disappointments too. His Derby mount,
Prince Charlemagne, proved to be a modest sort and he
finished out of the frame at Epsom. Mind you, it would have
taken a brave man to finish ahead of Gordon Richards that

day, for 1953 was the year of Pinza – the huge Murless-trained colt that gave the legendary jockey his first and only win in the big race. Poignantly, he had been knighted by the Queen days before the meeting, and on the run-in it was the Queen's own colt, Aureole, he passed. It was one of the easiest Derby wins for years and by far the most popular. Richards had been attempting to capture the supreme prize for the twenty-eighth time.

Not only did Richards win the Derby but England's cricketers won the Ashes, Stanley Matthews finally won an FA Cup winner's medal with Blackpool and Edmund Hillary conquered Mount Everest. British sportsmen scaled every pinnacle that year. It was a supreme and emotional time, especially with a new young Queen on the throne.

Lester's tally of winners dropped to forty-one, the lowest since his apprentice days. He finished fifteenth in the jockeys' table though his earnings dropped little, thanks to those two big wins at Epsom and Ascot. In the winter he took to hurdling once more but a crashing fall left him with a broken shoulder and the resulting period of inactivity was moodily spent.

It was, anyway, a winter calculated to depress the spirits. Mild for the most part, but invariably damp, it taxed the patience of owner and trainer alike as they sought to bring promising two-year-olds to peak fitness before the 1954 campaign. Joe Lawson was one such trainer. . .

4
Never Say Die

After fifty-odd years in racing, Joe Lawson had seen it all. He'd virtually won it all too, not as a jockey but as a trainer who, within four years of succeeding the legendary Alec Taylor at Manton in Leicestershire, had set an earnings record of £93,899. That was in 1931. The mark would not be eclipsed until 1957 when Noel Murless brought in £116,908 for his owners.

Still, Lawson had never won the Derby, a fact that niggled him as he moved into his seventies, an age when most men have long since retired to the golf course or the garden. His pursuit of the prize had even persuaded him to move to Newmarket, where, with a much reduced string, he continued to sift like a prospector for that single nugget of gold. In 1954, he thought he had found it, though few others shared his vision.

The colt in question was a big, rangy chestnut called Never Say Die. It had a useful pedigree – by champion stallion Nasrullah out of American-bred Singing Grass – but it showed little form as a two-year-old. A solitary victory in the six-furlong Rosslyn Stakes at Ascot had been hard won and five other outings had produced just two third places. Still, Lawson persisted in nursing the animal towards Epsom and by the spring of 1954 he at least had some physical signs to encourage him. Never Say Die had wintered well.

Lawson decided to open his campaign at Liverpool in the Union Jack Stakes, and eighteen-year-old Lester Piggott was booked for the ride. Never Say Die ran green that day, finishing well behind the winner, Tudor Honey, from whom he was receiving 5 lb. The young jockey was far from impressed but agreed to take the ride again in the Free Handicap and was surprised to find his mount a warm favourite. The bookmakers agreed with Lawson – the animal was just backward.

And backward was how Never Say Die finished. He didn't even get into the first six. Piggott was bitterly disappointed. He just couldn't understand how this well-made colt who gave him such a good feel could perform so moderately against horses that were clearly below him in class. It must be the distance, thought the youngster. He must need a longer trip.

Lawson had reached much the same conclusion. The Free Handicap was run over six furlongs. It was too sharp. So the trainer next entered the colt for the Newmarket Stakes to be run over a mile and a quarter and this time he gave the ride to the vastly experienced Manny Mercer. Like Lester Piggott, Mercer was a jockey of great sensitivity and infinite patience. And, like Piggott, he possessed the priceless gift of being able to make horses run for him.

But not this time. At Newmarket, Mercer rode one of his rare stinkers and if ever a race contrived to disguise a horse's true potential, this was it. Starting at a chilly 20/1 after his no-show last time out, Never Say Die cantered for the first half-mile, bowling along at the back of the field as if it were a training spin. Mercer seemed almost to have gone to sleep, but then shook himself out of his torpor to such effect that, while Never Say Die passed the Bushes in last place, he came out of the Dip leading by a street.

It was not a very clever piece of riding. Mercer had, at a stroke, both nullified the animal's stamina and sent him into the final two furlongs critically unbalanced. He was caught easily on the run-in by Elopement and Golden God and obliged to settle for a very shaky third place. Lawson shrugged. Every jockey has his off-day. The important thing was that this had not been a true-run race. He'd seen enough of Never Say Die to feel here was Derby-winning material.

Never Say Die's American owner, Robert Sterling Clark,

was not so sure. He was happy for the colt to run at Epsom but unwilling to cancel plans to spend Derby week in a New York nursing home. Like Lawson, the industrialist was in his early seventies, and while they had shared many a triumph together – including the 1,000 Guineas and Oaks with Galatea II – Clark had no obsessive desire to win the Derby. It would be nice – no more.

Following his eccentric Newmarket run, there was no great enthusiasm for Never Say Die in the Derby market (he would forego the 2,000 Guineas) and 33/1, even 40/1, was freely available. There were few takers, and even less a few days later when a curious story appeared in the *Daily Sketch*. In an interview with John Rickman, Clark's racing manager, Captain McElligot, expressed doubts about Never Say Die for the big race. 'He hangs to the right,' he told Rickman, 'and that will never do for a left-handed course like Epsom.'

The bookmakers took the hint and Never Say Die 'took a walk in the market', drifting out to 200/1 with the clear implication that he would be a non-runner. Lawson saw the story and phoned McElligot in a panic. 'Hey, you've got to run him in the Derby,' he said. 'The colt doesn't hang to the right, he hangs to the left and that will suit him down to the ground for Epsom.'

So Never Say Die stayed in by the skin of its teeth and a sheepish Lawson was left to explain the confusion. 'It was largely my fault,' he admitted. 'I inadvertently misinformed Captain McElligot.' Still the bookmakers and the betting public remained unimpressed, although Never Say Die did at least return to the fold at 33/1.

Now the trainer had to find a jockey, preferably one experienced around Epsom and able to ride to orders. If Never Say Die possessed one asset it was stamina and Lawson didn't want to see the colt's finish leak away in a helter-skelter dash around Tattenham Corner. Manny Mercer was his first choice, despite the débâcle at Newmarket, but the jockey was already booked for one of the favourites, 7/1 shot Darius. Four other jockeys were approached and one by one they were crossed off the list. Then Lawson thought of Lester Piggott.

Booking Lester, though, might prove a problem. Lawson had no qualms about the youngster's ability but he was painfully aware of the jockey's lack of enthusiasm for Never Say Die. So he decided to try a little subtle psychology. Lawson composed a telegram which read simply: 'YOU RIDE NEVER SAY DIE STOP STILL SORE ABOUT LOSING ON GAY TIME TO SMIRKE QUERY'.

He hit the target right on the button. Lester *was* still sore about that 1952 Derby defeat because, whichever way he carved it, he still came up with the same conclusion – it had been his fault. Even at eighteen, Piggott was judging himself by standards far above his fellow-men.

After all the false starts and scares, Lawson was entitled to feel satisfied just getting his horse to post with a jockey on its back. But still he nurtured grander dreams and, after working the colt a couple of times over the Derby distance at Newmarket, he had one last try at persuading Robert Sterling Clark to come over. The owner was apologetic, but the answer was still no. Lawson sighed, and replaced the receiver. He must carry his dream to Epsom alone.

Derby day dawned grey and cold. A raw wind swept the downs, straining the flags on the grandstand and chilling the huddled revellers in their open-topped charabancs.

There was a certain coolness in the Piggott household, too. For weeks Lester had been insisting that the big chestnut colt with the long stride had 'no chance'. It was a point of crackling irritation for father Keith as he drove his son the fifty miles from Lambourn to Epsom. 'He was very miserable,' said his father. 'When I asked him why he was so glum he just said, "He isn't good enough."'

The book agreed with Lester. Rowston Manor and Ferriol were installed as joint favourites at 5/1. Next came 2,000 Guineas winner Darius at 7/1 with Elopement, ridden by Piggott's *bête noire*, Charlie Smirke, at 9/1. After Valerullah, the Queen's Landau and Blue Sail, you could have had 25/1 upwards on the other fifteen, with Never Say Die at 33/1.

Finally, the Piggott Alvis arrived on the high downs and Lester climbed stiffly from the back seat. The sky had cleared a little, its greyness seeming to milk all colour from the swirling Derby Day crowd. After the excitement of Coronation Year and Gordon Richards's emotional win on Pinza, the champagne now seemed a little flat. Yet the tempo altered noticeably when the young Queen Elizabeth, accompanied by the Queen Mother and Sir Winston Churchill, stepped into the paddock to inspect the runners. Landau, appropriately, looked a picture but it was Arabian Night that took the eye.

They were off at 3.36, six minutes behind schedule, but they were off cleanly and fast. Moonlight Express took up the early running before yielding after a furlong and a half to the free-running Rowston Manor with Landau and Alpenhorn tucked in close behind. The gallop was unsettlingly quick, but Lester, remembering Joe Lawson's instructions, kept Never Say Die just off the pace.

As they swung down into Tattenham Corner, Rowston Manor stil held the lead but was beginning to blow and it was no surprise when Landau took up the running entering the straight. A mighty cheer went up from the grandstand as the Queen's colours came clearly into view with Manny Mercer, working furiously on Darius, barely a stride behind them.

Then came another, even bigger roar as Lester Piggott began to unfurl a run on Never Say Die. The colt quickened perceptibly, stretching those long legs into an all-consuming stride. Landau cracked, so did Darius and suddenly, within the final furlong, there was only one horse in it. Behind him, Lester could hear just a muted drumbeat as Arabian Night and Elopement pounded up the hill. It was in the bag, and he knew it.

The only sound Joe Lawson could hear was the thunderous pounding of his heart. His fingers were icy white on binoculars he no longer needed as his horse swept imperiously over the line. It was a stupendous triumph.

Never Say Die's two-lengths margin of victory over Arabian Night was highly flattering to the runner-up. It might easily have been ten. Darius took third place by a neck.

Lester Piggott, at eighteen years and six months, had become the youngest jockey ever to win the Derby, and Lawson the oldest trainer. Epsom was awash with emotion, an emotion shared by the young Queen who had seen her own hopes die as swiftly as a summer storm on that stamina-sapping run-in. Afterwards, Lester Piggott was as cool and clinical in his assessment of the race as he had been in his riding of it.

'I was fifth or sixth all the way,' he said, 'and at Tattenham Corner I was fifth and going very well among a bunch of other horses. A furlong later I deprived Darius of the lead and from that point I knew I should not be beaten. I just went for my life. I was never in any danger.'

Most of the jockeys blamed the firm going for torpedoing their hopes. American star Johnny Longden told the press, 'I have no excuse except to say that in my opinion Blue Sail did not like the firm going. At the time I began to fade I could see that the Queen's colt Landau was not liking it either, and he too went back.'

Said Rowston Manor's jockey Doug Smith: 'He didn't lengthen his stride in the straight as he did at Lingfield and I think this was because of the firm going.' Bill Nevett (Court Splendour): 'He went well to Tattenham Corner but didn't act on the course.' And Charlie Smirke, who had deprived Lester of victory on Tulyar two years before: 'He just fell down the hill.'

Lester listened but said nothing. He seemed, if anything, even more withdrawn and remote than on that prickly drive to the course. Instead, his father spoke for him as Fleet Street besieged the Piggott camp. 'Really, I think he was very elated but then, he never showed his feelings about anything. He knew how many hours he had put in to get where he has. He felt deep down that he deserved his success.'

In New York, Robert Sterling Clark was a stunned and happy man when news of his triumph reached him at the nursing home. Soon the wires from London were buzzing. 'This is the culmination of my thirty years of breeding,' he told the press, 'and I'm utterly overwhelmed.' And no, he added, he did not make a killing on the race. He was not a betting man. Never Say Die carried not a penny.

Back in London, leading bookmakers were describing it as 'the worst Derby in fifty years for the punters'. Two days before the race, more than £100,000 was lost by backers when Infatuation and Ambler II were scratched. Only the ebullient William Hill, who had briefly installed Never Say Die at 200/1 during the earlier confusion, had mixed feelings. 'My ante-post department pay out £168,000,' he said, but then added, 'It is still a good result for the books.'

Summing up that historic race thirty years later, Richard Baerlein of *The Guardian* is able to make an objective assessment of both horse and rider.

Never Say Die was a good horse, and funnily enough I had a big tickle on him. I was quite friendly with Joe Lawson and took due note when he ran Never Say Die in the Union Jack Stakes at Liverpool, a race which in those days often got a classic horse. And he looked a nice animal, always. But of course he was backward and until his stamina came into the picture he wasn't any good.

He *was* a surprise Derby winner though he had run well in the Newmarket Stakes – but I won't say I picked him [for his newspaper]. I went for Darius,which didn't stay. Nor would I say Never Say Die rated all that highly in Piggott's canon of Derby winners. The horses against it weren't all that good. The real significance of it was that it was his first Derby winner, and he got a lot of publicity through it. He rode a good race but I mean, I could probably have won on it. It simply outstayed the opposition.

That seems about right, and given Lester's perfectionist nature, probably accounts for his post-race reticence more accurately than either shyness or immaturity in his cool handling of the ensuing ballyhoo. And ballyhoo there certainly was.

Fleet Street sports editors practically drowned in their own dictionaries as they sought for superlatives to describe the new *Wunderkind* of the track. 'The Golden Boy', a tag bestowed on him at fourteen, would no longer do. 'Genius' seemed a bit extreme, but it was trotted out anyway along with eulogizing profiles as Britain suddenly found itself with a new sporting hero.

Yet their hero was practically monosyllabic. Words were like limpets prised from a rock, and even if you collected lots, they still didn't add up to a meal. It was perplexing for the serious racing journalist, heart-breaking for the feature writer. It is no wonder the hyperbole took over. The myths about Lester Piggott were certainly forged around this time, but while the portraits were essentially shadowy, some did manage to convey a little of the double-sided nature of the young jockey: on the one hand reckless, on the other heroic. Robin Goodfellow wrote in the *Daily Mail*, in a typical piece of the time:

> Never Say Die! That's it. Lester has many times felt the sting of words of older men trying to 'help' him. They have never got him down, that lad, who, let's face it, has at times been foolish. Suspensions – half a dozen of them: falls, about a dozen of them – bringing at least one broken leg: nothing has cowed this lad whom some call just 'plain obstinate' but whose spirit I have always admired.
>
> Like the great Fred Archer, once Lester is in the saddle he knows no fear. Daring, sometimes to the extent of rashness, he is so determined to win that he has been known to forget the orders given to him by his employer – owner or trainer. That is excusable. He is a boy. A year ago he was little more than a child. Obedience to instructions is, as any parent knows, just one of those things children do not learn in a day.

It was easy to see why already in the fifties the public had taken him to their hearts. 'Dashing', 'determined' – these words were like music to the ears of any punter, and couple that with a kind of romantic shyness that hinted of deeper things and it was equally easy to see why he had built such a female following.

After the hurly-burly of Epsom and the excesses of Fleet Street came a fortnight of comparative calm. The domestic caravan that is horse-racing moved onwards and outwards, gobbling up small towns like Stockton and Redcar,

Chepstow and Windsor, before regrouping on 16 June for the summer showpiece, Royal Ascot.

Piggott was to partner Never Say Die again in the King Edward VII Stakes, and again, Joe Lawson had prepared his charge to perfection. Its coat gleamed and there was a new spring in its stride as it pranced towards the paddock. Piggott couldn't have been happier. All doubts about the animal's ability had vanished in the hectic final seconds of Derby Day. Now, amidst the famous and the fashionable, Never Say Die was dressed for a coronation.

The King Edward VII Stakes is run over the Derby distance of one and a half miles, but there the similarity ends. Ascot is a right-handed, triangular course with a short finishing straight – so short, in fact, that if a horse is not well up to the pace coming out of the stiff climb up from Swinley Bottom, its chance is virtually nil. As Piggott himself has said, 'It's almost impossible to come from very far behind to win.'

But in other ways, Ascot suited Never Say Die better than Epsom. The horse thrived on a good gallop and Ascot is very much a galloping course. Its action may have been better suited to a left-handed track, but few in the huge crowd doubted its ability to make the necessary adjustment. Certainly not Joe Lawson or Lester Piggott.

Still, Lester knew he would have his work cut out keeping the big colt balanced and, to make life harder, he was conceding eight pounds in weight to the Derby runner-up Arabian Night, already being touted as a possible St Leger winner. Arabian Night was actually installed as favourite at 13/8 with Never Say Die 7/4 and Rashleigh, the Noel Murless hope ridden by Sir Gordon Richards, 5/1. It was a quality field. It had all the makings of a quality race. Instead, it became the most notorious in history.

After thirty years, tempers have cooled, wounds have healed, but the interpretation of what truly occurred on that June afternoon remains the subject for hot debate. *The Times* simply reported the facts:

> As the horses came round the turn into the straight, Rashleigh (Sir G. Richards) and Garter (W. Rickaby)

received bumps which nearly put them on the floor. Never
Say Die, with L. Piggott up, had been pocketed on the outside of these two. Halfway up the straight Blue Prince II and
Arabian Night were racing together in front. Arabian Night
crossed rather quickly from the outside position to the rails,
and a moment later swerved right out towards Blue Prince II
again. Meanwhile, Sir Gordon Richards on Rashleigh, pursued by Tulyar's brother, Tarjoman, came up on the outside
to win.

Those 'bumps' which *The Times* so clinically described
brought both Gordon Richards and Lester Piggott before the
stewards. Richards was exonerated immediately and
Rashleigh allowed to keep the race. Piggott was stood down
for the rest of the meeting and, ominously, further reported
to the stewards of the Jockey Club.

So what happened? I have read many versions but the two
that seem most authentic – contradicting one another but
each highly plausible – appear in Tim Fitzgeorge Parker's
biography of Murless, *The Guvnor*. First, Gordon Richards:

Coming into the straight, Blue Prince and Dragonfly were
making the running, with Rickaby on Garter third, Gosling
on Arabian Night fourth and I was fifth. Dragonfly dropped
out and I began to move up to the leader. All of a sudden,
Lester Piggott on Never Say Die started to make a move. I
was on the outside, so I do not know whether Never Say Die
was hanging or not. Lester claimed he was. At any rate,
Never Say Die charged into Garter, hit my quarters and
practically turned me around. Then Never Say Die charged
Garter again, and Garter turned me broadside on. I suspect
that it did look from the stands as if my horse was doing the
damage; but if another horse hits yours in the rump, it will
throw you into him, and that's what happened.

Rashleigh recovered marvellously and he and Tarjoman
went on to challenge Arabian Night who had taken up the
running with Blue Prince. Arabian Night dived twice, first of
all putting Blue Prince on to Tarjoman and then Tarjoman
on to me. But Rashleigh would not be beaten whatever happened to him and he went on to win. Of course, it was a most
unsatisfactory race and the Stewards objected to me. But

immediately they had heard the evidence, they withdrew their objection. They did, however, stand Lester Piggott down.

Lester's account was:

I was lying handy on the rails. As there were three horses in front of me, who were beginning to weaken, I decided to switch to the outside to give my horse a long unimpeded run with that great style of his. As I started to move, however, one of the leaders dropped back and at that moment, Gordon came from behind further outside and proceeded to ride in. First, he lay on the other horse. Then, although looking across he could see I hadn't much room, he pushed the other horse right on top of me. Of course there was a big bump and the other horse was half turned. My horse was hanging towards his favourite left-hand side, which of course didn't help matters.

As soon as we got back the Stewards objected to Gordon – rightly, in my opinion – but, when they heard the evidence of the other jockeys, they withdrew their objection and turned their objection to me, claiming that I had been trying to force my way out.

With no camera patrol film to guide them in those days, the stewards were bound to rely heavily on the evidence of the jockeys and make their judgement accordingly. On the face of it, the evidence seems conflicting enough for all – or none – of the jockeys involved to have been stood down. But facing them that day were two contrasting figures: one, Sir Gordon Richards, a scion of the Turf, the darling of the Establishment; the other, the acknowledged 'bad boy' of racing, Lester Piggott. It was inevitable that Lester should lose out, which is not the same as saying he *was* the innocent party, merely that, when it comes to a lynching, truth and justice are the first things to go out of the window.

And there, perhaps, the matter should have ended. But it didn't. Piggott was further reported to the stewards of the Jockey Club in London, which is the rough equivalent of a magistrate committing the accused to stand trial at the Old

Bailey – though without benefit of a jury. Here, Lester's past record of suspensions and warnings would be regarded as a key factor in any judgement. As it proved.

To the shock of the whole racing community, Lester was suspended indefinitely and ordered to leave his apprenticeship with his father at Lambourn. The official statement read, in part:

> . . . Having taken notice of his dangerous and erratic riding both this season and in previous seasons and that in spite of continuous warnings he continued to show complete disregard for the Rules of Racing and the safety of other jockeys, before any application for a renewal of Piggott's licence can be entertained he must be attached to some other trainer than his father for a period of six months.

It was a savage sentence and it left the youngster hurt and bewildered. 'It is harsh and ridiculous,' he told the press. 'Now that my licence has been withdrawn indefinitely it means that I am barred from riding in trials. This has been a very great blow and I am very disappointed. I have no idea when I may be able to race again. It may be six months, it may be longer.'

Keith Piggott was equally upset, especially as in the broadest sense he was cast as the villain of the piece. 'Apparently the stewards think that I am in some way to blame. They told me that the boy will have to go to another trainer, which means, in effect, that he will have to leave home.'

That in itself proved to be less of a hardship. It was decided that Lester's indentures be transferred to Jack Jarvis at Newmarket and that he would lodge with his uncle, Fred Lane, and his cousin, Bill Rickaby. Jarvis was one of the most respected trainers in racing and it was felt that his experience and wisdom would have a beneficial influence on the youngster. It didn't quite work out like that. 'The old man was sick in bed the whole time I was there,' Lester revealed later, 'so that was a fat lot of good!' And, more bitterly, 'Six months hard bloody labour and less than a fiver a week while serving it.'

For a teenager whose income from racing had by now comfortably topped the £5,000 a year mark, that was a particularly harsh pill to swallow. Even harsher was the thought of the rides he would be missing, notably on Derby partner Never Say Die in the last classic of the season, the St Leger. And who should Joe Lawson choose for the ride? None other than Charlie 'What did I Tulyar' Smirke. The irony was profound.

But, once again, Piggott was to confound those critics who had made their value judgements on the 'reckless' young jockey and smugly closed the book. Lester knuckled down to work with a vengeance at Newmarket, and far from resenting Smirke's 'pinching' of his ride, he telephoned the jockey before the St Leger to advise the older man on just how Never Say Die should be ridden. Smirke was touched, and the new combination duly obliged with Lawson's second classic win of the season at 100/30. This time the owner too was present and immediately after the race he announced that the colt would be retired and stand at the National Stud. It was a fine gesture from a true anglophile, though one Joe Lawson accepted with bitter-sweet feelings. He felt Never Say Die had a brilliant future as a four-year-old, and he was probably right. But the question never arose, and, two years later, Clark died at the age of seventy-five. He never met Piggott.

Meanwhile, behind the scenes, Keith Piggott and others had been canvassing hard for Lester's release. For the most part, his behaviour at Newmarket had been impeccable. Hungry newshounds who had hoped to keep the pot boiling had been politely but firmly turned away. Piggott knew that he must play the game according to the Jockey Club's rules, however much he privately resented them. And then, in late August, came an incident that catapulted him back into the headlines.

At evening stables, Lester finished grooming his 'two' and returned the brushes to the saddle-room. As he left, another stable lad, 62-year-old Peter Kearns, approached Piggott and accused him of taking his brushes. An argument followed, then a scuffle and Kearns was left nursing a badly cut

But Gordon Richards, like other great riders before him, and even Lester Piggott today, was extremely reluctant to leave the saddle. His skill had hardly diminished after thirty-four years and, in fact, age and experience had added an extra dimension to his riding, an overview which enabled him to anticipate moves much earlier in a race. Neither had he become bored with the daily routine or blasé about the winnows he steered home. He was simply in love with the game and couldn't bear to leave it.

But then, on a cool July afternoon at Sandown Park, the decision was taken out of his hands. As Richards walked the filly Abergeldie up a gravel pathway to the stable yard, the animal suddenly reared up on its hind legs and flipped over, throwing the jockey to the ground. It was a moment so dramatic, so unexpected, that for a second onlookers seemed suspended with shock. Then, suddenly, everyone was rushing to aid.

Noel Murless, who was first onto the scene along with Richards's chauffeur, knew at once that the injuries were serious. The jockey's foot had become entangled in the stirrup so that the full weight of the animal had landed on him, as it flipped over, and then a second time as it struggled up. After what seemed an excessive delay, Richards was carried on a stretcher to the field ambulance and rushed twelve miles to Rowley Bristow Orthopaedic Hospital at Pyrford.

That night, his surgeon, Mr E. G. Slesinger, was able to issue a bulletin reassuring an anxious public that while 'Sir Gordon Richards's condition is serious, he is not in any danger. He has dislocated a bone of his pelvis and will not be able to ride again for at least two months.'

The impact of the accident was overwhelming. Cards, letters, telegrams, flowers poured into the hospital, and they came from every stratum of society. Even the Queen, staying at Windsor Castle for the weekend, sent a get-well message and asked to be kept informed of his condition. I doubt if any sportsman has been more popular in his time and it is easy to connect with that tidal wave of emotion, except through contemporary newspaper accounts and by

ear that required hospital treatment. The police were called, statements taken – and then the press moved in. At last they had a story.

Lester, nursing a dark bruise under his left eye, received them and gave his version of events.

'This and a cut inside my lip were what Kearns did to me,' he said. 'I didn't mean to hurt him – I was just defending myself. I had finished grooming one of my horses, and later, putting my tools away I must have taken Kearns's instead. He came storming up. I said I must have put them in the saddle-room by mistake. He went to the wrong saddle-room, then came back in a temper and hit me and cut my lip.

'I didn't want any trouble with a man so much older,' Piggott continued, 'so I walked away. He came after me and hit me again. I told him not to be daft over a thing like that, but he still wanted to fight. I pushed him away. Then he went off to the police.'

From his hospital bed, Kearns also came under scrutiny. 'He made me so angry that I clipped him one,' he said. 'I have told the police that. It was because of what happened afterwards that I went to the police.'

Lester summed up: 'I am hoping this will all blow over without spoiling my chances of riding again.'

It didn't. No charges were brought and Lester was once more able to dissolve into the background. Then, on 23 September, eleven days after the St Leger, all that behind the scenes campaigning paid off. The stewards relented, the ban was lifted. Lester Piggott was a licensed jockey again.

But it was one thing to be allowed to ride again, quite another to actually do it. During the months of inactivity, Lester's weight shot up to 9 st. 7 lb. It meant that for the first time he would have to experience the private hell called 'wasting'. Nothing in his young life had prepared him for that.

He had been booked to ride Cardington King at Newmarket in the autumn meeting and the race was only five days away. Somehow, he must shed a stone and a half and remain strong enough and alert enough to steer a racehorse at upwards of 40 miles an hour. He accepted the challenge with resignation and determination. He not only lost the weight but he turned Cardington King into a winner.

And then, quite suddenly, the season was over. There was much to reflect on. The final statistics added up to 42 winners from 262 rides and 18th place in the champion jockeys' table. Lester considered it a meagre tally for a year that had begun with such bright promise only to turn to ashes in his mouth. He vowed that he would never occupy such a lowly place again. He knew in his heart that he was now as good as, if not better than, his contemporaries. It was time to leave them all behind.

1955 couldn't come quickly enough. . .

5

The Murless Connection

During the long limbo of that summer spent i[n] yard, Lester found himself with plenty of tim[e] much time, perhaps, for a youngster with divert him. No motor bike to tinker with. N[o] only pleasure came from riding out in the [morn]ings and it was barely enough to sustain hi[m] was to say of that barren time, 'My life jus[t] racing is my whole life.'

It is easy to imagine how a brooding bit[terness] crept in. But Lester was too defiant for [that,] the point, too ambitious. Instead, like so[me] ter who sees the pattern of the game lo[ng ahead] was planning out the next moves in hi[s] those moves was to secure the top job[in the sta]bles in the land. He wanted to ride for [Murless.]

It may have seemed a precocious a[mbition, but] some substance. Murless's number o[ne jockey,] Sir Gordon Richards, still champio[n, was] beginning, however reluctantly, t[o think of] retirement. Richards had even take[n over Noel's] yards at Beckhampton and install[ed himself, to keep] the place ticking over. So the even[tuality was] not in question, only its timing.

talking to his friends. There is no doubt that Gordon Richards touched hearts and minds and did so in an era overflowing with charismatic sporting heroes.

The recovery was as slow and painful as his surgeon had said it would be. And while he lay strapped and immobile – there had also been four broken ribs – Richards found himself, like Lester Piggott, with much thinking time on his hands. He had accepted now that his racing career was over. There had been 4,870 triumphs in 21,834 races and 200 or more winners in 12 of his 26 championship seasons . . . and finally, and most memorably, there had been Pinza, his only Derby winner in twenty-eight attempts.

But still there was no sudden retirement announcement from Pyrford. Richards played poker with the press and the public as he considered his new career from a hospital bed. Earlier plans to purchase yearlings at the Newmarket July Auctions had been abandoned and it seemed he must wait until the Autumn Sales at Doncaster before he could begin filling his yard. In a sense, though, horses were the least of his problems. The immediate thing was to find a top-class stable jockey.

There were any number of promising youngsters around, with Piggott, Joe Mercer and Geoff Lewis perhaps the pick of the crop, along with 21-year-old Jock Wilson, who was building quite a reputation with trainer Staff Ingham. Richards was very much in favour of youth, though the experience of Eph Smith, middle brother of future champion jockey Doug Smith, also appealed. In the end, he decided to go for Piggott, the man he viewed as his most likely successor.

Lester was flattered by the great man's offer, but his eyes didn't exactly mist over. He felt he now had bigger fish to fry and it was Richards's old job at Warren Place that he coveted. He said No to Richards and instead put through a call to Noel Murless. 'You need a new jockey,' he said in effect. 'I'm your man.'

It is tempting to suggest that Lester's cheeky initiative got him the job, but it wasn't quite like that. Murless certainly admired his boldness, but he had already drawn up a short

list of three candidates, and the first name on that list was
Scobie Breasley.

The Australian had returned to England in 1953 to ride for
Noel Cannon, two years after abandoning his first foray into
British racing. It had taken a lot to tempt Breasley back from
his beloved Melbourne where he was a huge celebrity. But
then Cannon offered a lot, including the opportunity for
Breasley and his wife May to live in London if they wished
and only visit Cannon's Wiltshire stables to ride occasional
work. So Scobie had settled in Roehampton in an eccentri-
cally styled art-deco villa and soon became so attached to it,
and his new way of life, that when the call came from Murless
it came too late.

'For me, a comparative newcomer to English racing, to be
given the chance of stepping into Gordon's boots was
nothing short of an honour,' says Scobie in his autobiography. 'But I neither wanted to uproot my home again nor
travel up to Newmarket two or three days a week in order to
ride work.'

Manny Mercer was the second name on Murless's list, but
he too was attached – which left Lester, still under suspension and kicking his heels uselessly at Newmarket. Murless
had decided, after Breasley's refusal, to wait until the end of
the season when the horse-trading for retainers and positions
would have eased off and a clearer picture would emerge.
But Lester's call changed all that, while, in the meantime,
Willie Snaith, number two jockey at Warren Place, and
Charlie Smirke were given Richards's rides with Doug Smith
and Bill Rickaby occasionally filling in.

Finally, Lester was summoned to Warren Place and so
began the meeting which was to change the whole face of
English racing.

Murless, tall, courteous, stiff with a military bearing, and
Piggott, shy, awkward and far from articulate, hit it off at
once. Each sensed in the other an intense professionalism, a
dedication to success and a true understanding of the tools of
their trade – thoroughbred racehorses. There were no reservations and the meeting concluded with Murless offering
Lester what the jockey laconically described as, 'a very

worthwhile retainer'. Within days of his nineteenth birthday on 5 November, Lester had achieved his ambition. He was indeed top jockey at the top stable.

Just how rich was the seam of gold that Piggott had unearthed, quickly became clear to him. Murless's owners included the Queen, Prince Aly Khan, Sir Percy Loraine and, above all, Sir Victor Sassoon, who was to form the crucial third part of the Great Triumvirate. It would be Sassoon's Little Cloud that would provide the new jockey with his first winner of 1955 for the stable, although, with a delicious irony, Lester had ended 1954 by steering home Rashleigh – the Murless-trained colt that had brought about Lester's dramatic downfall.

With such a wealth of talent now at his disposal, Lester's tally of winners was to increase dramatically in 1955, from 42 to 103, good enough for third place in the championship table, topped by Doug Smith. And Lester might very well have landed his second classic winner in the St Leger but for some contentious ducking and diving on the run-in by the Oaks and 1,000 Guineas winner Meld.

This time Piggott was in the colours of Miss Dorothy Paget, a highly eccentric but ferociously wealthy spinster. Dorothy Paget had inherited a fortune and a passion for horse-racing, plus the occasional odd habit – like eating lunch at three o'clock in the morning and, if she took breakfast, starting it at tea-time. She frequently appeared on the racecourse in a huge, shapeless overcoat buttoned to the chin and with a cloche hat rammed firmly on her head. Her size was certainly intimidating and so was her tongue: Scobie Breasley was always referred to as 'that wretched Breasley', possibly a backhanded term of endearment but not one always readily appreciated by racegoers within range of her booming voice. Finally, she was a gambler of rare nerve, thinking nothing of laying out a six-figure sum on a horse she had a fancy for.

The horse Lester Piggott rode for her that day was Nucleus, an attractive animal but one with a temperament that belied his looks. He could be sour, he could be aggressive, and Lester knew he had a challenge on his hands just getting the colt to post. But, equally, he knew it was a challenge he could handle.

Meld was the clear favourite, although she was a filly and fillies usually come off second best against the colts. But the fact was that she was an outstanding racehorse, one of the best of the century, and came to Doncaster with the Triple Crown in her sights after walking off with the 1,000 Guineas and Oaks. Some paddock observers wondered if she was quite right with herself as she paraded in the ring, but doubts were soon forgotten when, after a funereal first three-quarters of a mile, she moved smoothly to the head of the field with Beau Prince.

Coming into the straight, Beau Prince challenged Meld on the outside only for the filly to step up a gear and establish what seemed from the stands to be a winning lead. But finishing fast was Lester Piggott on Nucleus. Meld's jockey Harry Carr got to work with his whip, but the filly was tiring badly and each time he hit her she veered closer and closer to the rails.

Lester Piggott, like some predatory shark, had got the first whiff of blood and as Meld began to go walkabout he shook Nucleus up. But the colt didn't like the whip one bit and jinked sharply to the left behind the favourite. Meld was, by now, just hanging on, but even though Carr had put down his whip, the animal continued to drift leftwards, leaving Lester with no choice but to switch Nucleus to the outside. The move came too late. Nucleus couldn't quite make up the ground and Meld hung on by three-quarters of a length with Beau Prince finishing a tired third.

Lester was furious. He practically leapt off his animal's back and then stalked straight to the weighing room, borrowed £10 from a fellow jockey and promptly lodged an objection. He hadn't waited to consult Charles Jerdein, who held the licence on behalf of the stable controlled by Mrs Johnson Houghton (officially, there were no women trainers allowed in those days), and the stewards, perhaps a little put out by Piggott's peremptory manner, quickly threw the objection out of court. He was also ordered to forfeit his deposit.

It was hard luck on the jockey, who felt cheated by the result and miffed at not getting what he considered a proper hearing. Most experienced observers that day believe Nucleus was an unlucky loser. Had he maintained a straight run when Lester used the whip, it is possible he might have got up on the line. On the other hand, he might not. You never knew quite where you were with Nucleus, and the sad sequel to his career was that he died of a brain tumour the following season after landing three good victories. The illness undoubtedly explains his sour disposition.

Dorothy Paget had not been at Doncaster to see her colt run, but had she been, she would probably have backed Piggott's protest. She, like a growing number of influential owners, was a great admirer of Murless's new stable jockey who rode with such skill and vigour. He rode, too, with a judgement of pace that was mature well beyond his years. In bringing home the 11/10 favourite Darius for Harry Wragg in the Eclipse Stakes, Lester rode the kind of finish only he could achieve.

For Lester, the year ended as it had begun with a winner for Sir Victor Sassoon, this time on Kandy Sauce in the Queen Bess Plate at Birmingham. Murless had saddled thirty-six winners, but the winnings stakes of £23,065 served to emphasize just how important a classic winner can be to the economics of a big stable. There hadn't been one in 1955. Nor would 1956 be any better, though forty-seven races would be won. But for Murless, softly, softly was the name of the game, and having at the beginning of 1955 taken over management of Sassoon's studs, he knew precisely what was in the pipeline. So did Lester. The rest of the racing world was in for a shock.

6 | Crepello

The Watchers on the Heath, those weathered sleuths of the racing press whose job it is to assess the fitness and potential of racehorses at work, had eyes for just one animal in the warm spring of 1957. It was a big, handsome chestnut colt with a turn of foot that could blur the vision and turn somersaults with the imagination. His name was Crepello.

He had ran just twice as a two-year-old, beaten a short head by the speedy Fulfer in the Windsor Castle Stakes at Royal Ascot in June 1956 and then on 1 November providing Noel Murless with his final winner of the 1956 season in the seven-furlong Dewhurst Stakes at Newmarket.

On the first outing, Crepello was green enough for the trainer to give firm handling instructions to his jockey. 'Whatever happens, don't touch him with the whip, don't even show it to him.' Lester obeyed, although the temptation to give the colt just a tiny reminder on the furious run-in must have been overwhelming. But patience was to prove the overriding hallmark in turning Crepello into a great champion. Soon after that debut race, Murless detected what he described as 'the tiniest little notch, not as big as the end of a match, under his suspensory'. But he knew at once that the colt might be vulnerable, and no stable lad was ever allowed to feel the animal's rather straight forelegs while Crepello was in training.

Indeed, so sure was Murless of the animal's potential that his detailed preparation led him to have a pair of cloth bandages sewn on to those brittle forelegs. Every time the Watchers took up station on the Newmarket gallops they had little difficulty in picking out the chestnut from the 2,000 or more animals at exercise. There was no need to refer to the meticulously crafted workbooks with their dots and dashes and crosses which provide a unique and foolproof identification of the markings of each and every one.

But Murless had more than one trump in the Warren Place pack in the spring of '57. There was, too, the Victor Sassoon filly Suija which seemed a live 1,000 Guineas candidate. Piggott rode her to perfection in the Fred Darling Stakes at Newbury and a fortnight later was on the Queen's Carrozza in the Princess Elizabeth Stakes at Epsom.

Lester's report of Carrozza's running that day confirmed a picture already taking shape in the trainer's mind. The fifteen-hands, once backward filly had grown into a sprightly, well-balanced performer and might be just the right candidate for the Oaks. The Guineas was another matter and Lester can be forgiven for thinking that Suija was the better bet in that tricky race. As it happened, Rose Royale II proved better than either of them on the day, although Lester, well adrift on Suija, was impressed with Carrozza's fourth place performance in the hands of his cousin Bill Rickaby.

In any case, he had reason enough to be satisfied. Two days earlier he had taken Crepello, second favourite at 7/2 behind Pipe of Peace, to the start of the 2,000 Guineas and gone on to ride one of his most sensitive winning races. Sensitive, because there was a huge question mark over Crepello's soundness that day. The racing press, noting the exceptional firmness of the ground, had wondered aloud – and in unison – if the big colt's suspect forelegs could handle the going. Piggott nursed his mount, staying up with the pace but out of the lead until two hundred yards from home. Then he let Crepello fly and he was still flying as Quorum and Pipe of Peace tried to come at him going up the hill. The official distance was half a length and a head, but as Murless later noted, 'If Lester had let him down, it could so easily have been 10 lengths.'

So Crepello returned sound and ready to fight another

day, while Piggott had carved the second notch on his totem of classics. The Derby would soon follow.

But still the rumours persisted. This time, a new dimension was added. In those harum-scarum days when doping, real or imagined, was almost the topic of the racing day, Crepello found himself being nobbled in the press. A conspiracy had been hatched to 'get at' the Derby favourite before the off and Murless was obliged to step up security at Warren Place. It was the last thing he needed.

Crepello continued to perform well on the gallops, even at flat out over the Derby distance of one and a half miles, but nagging at the back of the trainer's mind was always that suspect suspensory. In his biography of Murless, Tim Fitzgeorge Parker spells out those worries.

> The going on that undulating, one and a half mile Derby course was hard and rough, with broken bottles on the track. With the roads and paths that he had to cross it was a nightmare for a bad-legged horse. Perhaps the worst hazard of all was the tarmac road, crossing the course by the pub a hundred yards past the winning post. This was covered with a light sprinkling of tan or dirt but was disturbed between every race by pedestrians and traffic. Any classic colt that had given his utmost in the greatest test of his life would be starting to pull up, still leading on his near foreleg when he came to this road and inevitably he would lean towards his stables over on the right and change with a sickening jar onto his off-fore. The number of horses in those days that developed leg trouble after running the Derby must have been legion.

Strangely, the bookmakers chose to ignore rumours of Crepello's possible unsoundness and when Derby day arrived he opened the market at 11/4 – a price that quickly hardened to 6/4 at first sight of him in the paddock. The animal was clearly tuned to the minute and his jockey seemed as relaxed and easy as if this were to be just an afternoon hack.

Another to catch the eye was the 33/1 outsider Ballymoss, a medium-sized chestnut colt trained in Ireland by Vincent O'Brien. After winning everything it was possible to win under National Hunt rules – including a hat-trick of Gold Cups and Grand Nationals – O'Brien had finally decided to turn his attention to the Flat. This was his first season and Ballymoss his first classic candidate. Had more been known of his homework, especially his crushing victory over stable companion and red-hot favourite Gladness in Ireland's Trigo Stakes, it is certain that Ballymoss would have gone to post well regarded. But Crepello's apparent greatness had thrown a smokescreen over everything. The Derby market was uneven and there was a suspicion that there were more than a few really poor horses in the field for the premier classic.

Twenty-two runners went to post and the start was messy. It took two attempts to bring the field into line and when the tapes did go up the second favourite, Prince Taj, whipped round to be left six lengths. Crepello, drawn number two, got away smoothly and Lester was able to place him handily in second place on the rails as the field climbed towards the mile post. Outside Lester was the American-owned Bois de Miel, one of the animals considered well below standard for the race, and sure enough, after half a mile, the colt cracked, leaving faster horses galloping all over the course as they fought to avoid the exhausted animal.

Lester was aware of the commotion behind him but mercifully immune. The inside draw had allowed him to choose exactly the position and pace he wanted and now, as the field regrouped and swung down into Tattenham Corner, he had settled Crepello in sixth, still on the rails.

There was more banging and bumping as the leading runners became bunched up, but as they turned into the home straight daylight magically appeared and each of the fancied contenders had a clear run for home. Ballymoss, with T. P. Burns working furiously on his back, made the initial break for the line a quarter of a mile from home. But Lester, out in the centre of the course, had the move well covered and brought Crepello smoothly up to the lead as they entered the final furlong.

Ballymoss had no answer. The Murless colt cut down the leader within a few strides and Lester was able to drop his hands in the final fifty yards as Crepello eased home. Ballymoss stayed on well to be second, a length clear of the fast-finishing Pipe of Peace. Last was Bois de Miel, whose entry came in for scornful criticism from jockeys who felt that their animals had been deprived of their true running.

The Queen's jockey Harry Carr fumed: 'I have never ridden in a rougher Derby, although I must make it clear that no jockey indulged in rough riding. In fact, they did their utmost to avoid trouble. But just after half a mile Bois de Miel faltered suddenly and half a dozen horses could not avoid the resulting scramble. Mine was one of them. He was knocked right out of his stride.'

Australian Rae Johnstone on Chippendale II said, 'My horse could not get out of the way in time and was knocked right back.' Bill Rickaby, agreeing with the other jockeys' summing up, added, 'The gallop was a slow one and a lot of the trouble may have been due to this.' In fact, it was the fastest Derby win since Mahmoud's record-shattering run in 1936!

As Lester brought Crepello into the unsaddling enclosure he was surprised to find the colt's owner, Sir Victor Sassoon, waiting to take his winner's rein. Sassoon had suffered appalling injuries in a flying accident in his youth and was usually confined to a wheel-chair when he went to the races. But so thrilled was he by Lester's performance that afternoon that he made a supreme effort to walk and greet the champion with the aid of a walking stick. It was a gesture Piggott was never to forget and there was nothing wintry about his smile that chilly afternoon.

The press were unstinting in their praise. At twenty-one, Lester had truly come of age in the eyes of those observers who had thrilled to the many triumphs of Gordon Richards and, even earlier, of that other great genius, Steve Donoghue. Murless, too, was showered with accolades for the brilliant way he had prepared the colt. In the euphoric moment, Sassoon was quick to announce that Crepello would be aimed at the St Leger in an attempt to become the first Triple Crown winner since Barham in 1935. And Noel Murless knew that once again he would have to perform a training miracle.

But it was to Lester Piggott that the next miracle attempt was to fall, just two days later in the Oaks when he climbed aboard the Queen's Carrozza in search of an Epsom double.

The Queen had two runners in the race and it was in fact Mulberry Harbour, trained at Freemason Lodge by the great Captain Cecil Boyd Rochford, that wore the first colours. The favourite was Guineas winner Rose Royale II with French jockey Jean Massard aboard. Another well-fancied candidate was Silken Glider, trained in Ireland by Seamus McGrath and ridden by Jimmy Eddery, father of Pat Eddery. Finally, there was Tattinger carrying Sir Victor Sassoon's colours once more and entrusted to the Australian, Edgar Britt.

Once again, Lester Piggott made a perfect break at the start and Carrozza was lying a handy fourth as the field swung down into Tattenham Corner with Tattinger just showing in the lead from Mulberry Harbour. Into the straight, the Queen's main hope began to fade and so too did Tattinger. Lester was on the rails and as Britt's mount weakened it hung slightly to the right, leaving a handy gap which Lester exploited in a flash. Carrozza shot to the front.

With two furlongs to go, the favourite Rose Royale II ran out of steam, but at the same moment Jimmy Eddery unleashed a run on Silken Glider. For a moment, Carrozza was headed but, game filly that she was, she immediately fought back and as they came up the hill to the winning post she again nudged her nose in front. It was thrilling stuff.

Silken Glider and Carrozza passed the stands together and the judge immediately called for a photograph. On the rails, the bookmakers were laying 7/4 against the Queen's filly and Lester Piggott's morose expression seemed to confirm that view. Then came the announcement: 'Carrozza by a short head'. The cheer that erupted threatened to lift the roof off the grandstand.

So at twenty-one Piggott had pulled off the coveted Epsom double and Noel Murless had saddled his third successive classic winner.

Afterwards, debate over the verdict would rage long and loud, but in the end there was always the evidence of the magic eye to settle the argument. Jimmy Eddery, in Claude

Duval's biography of his son, Pat Eddery, remembers it this way: 'Silken Glider was a top class filly but was a very difficult ride. Without wishing to be unkind, she was in fact a bit of a bitch. Still, I fancied her to land the Oaks. People always say that the greatest race Lester Piggott ever rode was that day and I can vouch for that. Christ, you never saw a man get so much out of a horse that day. He was really inspired and it was just my luck to meet him in that mood.'

Lester Piggott says: 'Carrozza was only tiny and a bit lazy but she was as game as a pebble. She was dying in the last hundred yards, but she gave everything she had and as we passed the post I didn't know whether we had held on or not. I do know that a couple of strides after passing the post, Jimmy Eddery was definitely in front.'

Eddery again: 'I was certain I had won. It was one of the very first times that a camera was in operation for the finish and I was happy and pretty certain I had got the nod. Lester Piggott thought he had lost and so did Noel Murless. But Seamus McGrath thought that we had just lost and he was right. To this day I still think it was very debatable, although I have never actually seen the photograph. It would bring back unhappy memories. I only really lost because Silken Glider was such a difficult mare to ride in the final stages.'

Noel Murless: 'I think it was the most brilliant race of Lester's entire career.'

Sir Gordon Richards, finally: 'Just think of it . . . he was only 21 . . . riding for the Queen . . . and it was the Oaks. But it made no difference to Lester. He behaved just as if it had been a selling race and, at precisely the right moment, before the other jockeys knew what was happening, he went. Believe me, he stole that race.'

On the face of it, there seemed to be nothing but blue skies for Piggott and Murless as they set out to annex further big prizes in that fabulous 1957 season. But there were dark clouds on the horizon, both physically and metaphorically, and it was to be that magnificent animal Crepello in the eye of the storm.

After Epsom, Murless was determined to give the Derby winner a good, long rest. His plan was to run the colt in the

Great Voltigeur Stakes at York preparatory to his Triple Crown attempt in the St Leger in September. But Crepello was also a provisional entry for the rich King George VI and Queen Elizabeth Stakes at Royal Ascot and the racing press assumed he would fulfil that engagement first. Betting on the horse was heavy and persistent and it was to lead to embarrassment and even rancour.

With the press stirring up Crepello fever with each succeeding article, Murless found himself in something of a cleft stick. He had no other runner for Sir Victor Sassoon at Royal Ascot and, finally, he felt obliged to let him run for the sake of the ageing owner and the betting public. But on 20 July the weather turned skittish. Summer storms swept across southern England and Ascot was deluged by rain an hour before the start of the meeting. The going, once good to firm, quickly became soft, and finally – and fatally – heavy.

Lester Piggott rode Aorangi in the opening race and returned to tell the trainer and owner, 'the going is too heavy for Crepello'. Sassoon consulted Murless and was quickly persuaded that the colt should be withdrawn. When the non-runner board went up against Crepello's number, the crowd were at first shocked and then angry. Any number of possible winners had missed this, the richest engagement of the season, simply because of Crepello's presence. In the end, victory went to a 20/1 French outsider, which did little to mollify the spectators.

Lester took the storm – both storms – in his customary detached, shoulder-shrugging way. He was sorry for the punters, of course, but then he was also sorry for himself. After all, it was his 10 per cent of a possible winning prize of £30,000 that was now rushing down the drain with a tide of torn betting slips. The important thing was that Crepello should be sound for the St Leger.

Sadly, though, Crepello did not remain sound. As Murless prepared him for that tune-up in the Great Voltigeur Stakes, the horse began to go in those suspect forelegs and the next dramatic announcement from the Warren Place team was that Crepello would never run again. So the wonder horse of the late 1950s was reluctantly retired to stud.

There were to be no more super horses for Piggott to ride that summer, although major prizes continued to come his way. Pin Sheel and Pinched provided useful consolations for both owner and trainer at Goodwood and Ascot, and at season's end Lester could reflect on a winning tally of 122 while Murless became champion trainer for the second time with a record £116,908 earned for his owners. He also became the first man to break the £100,000 barrier.

It was perhaps inevitable that there should be some sort of reaction the following year. But although there were no classic winners in 1958, there were some marvellous victories, most notably in the long-distance races at which Lester was to become the acknowledged master. He landed the Chester Cup (2 m. 2 f.) for the first time on Sandiacre at a handy 15/2 and then teamed up with Vincent O'Brien's great stayer, Gladness, to win the Ascot Gold Cup (2 m. 4 f.), the Goodwood Cup (2 m. 5 f.) and the Tote Ebor (1 m. 6 f.) at York. Ballymoss made it a brilliant year for the Irish trainer by landing the Prix de l'Arc de Triomphe at Longchamp and thus crowning O'Brien's conversion to the Flat after years of undiluted success under National Hunt rules. The Piggott–O'Brien combination had been seen in harness for the first time.

Lester ended the 1958 season on eighty-three winners, slipping to sixth in the jockeys' table. Murless's fall was somewhat greater. He managed to saddle just twenty-five winners for a total of £24,331 in stakes. But for both men there was a star on the horizon: a little grey filly named Petite Etoile after her sire, Petition, and dam, Star of Iran. She was to be slow coming to hand, but when she did, she was to take the racing world by storm.

7
Petite Etoile

It is rare for Lester Piggott to misjudge the potential of any animal he has ridden. It has happened, most notably in 1983 with All Along which cost him perhaps a million dollars in total earnings. But his initial failure to grasp Petite Etoile's future was nothing more than just bad luck.

Murless entered the 1959 season knowing that he again had a strong hand. 1958 would be seen as merely a hiccup on the graph of excellence which was to spiral onwards and upwards for another eight years. The two-year-olds had developed nicely, especially the Sassoon-owned filly Collyria and the Queen's Short Sentence. Prince Aly Khan had taken over the running of his father's horses following the Aga Khan's death at the age of eighty and his French trainer, Alec Head, had engaged the brilliant Australian George Moore to ride for him in France.

According to Murless, Aly Khan had sights on both the 2,000 and 1,000 Guineas and he was anxious to give Moore experience over the Newmarket course before the big events. So he asked Murless to put Moore up on one of his runners in the Free Handicap. The trainer had both Short Sentence and Petite Etoile booked for the race but felt Moore should not be given the ride on the Queen's horse and instead should partner Petite Etoile. The grey filly trotted up by three lengths and Murless began to suspect classic potential.

Lester, meanwhile, had grown used to working Collyria on the gallops and when Murless offered him the choice of mounts for the Guineas he decided to stick with the known quantity. So champion jockey Doug Smith was given the ride. Petite Etoile blitzed the field.

She went to the post third favourite at 8/1 but soon made a mockery of those odds as Smith struggled to hold her coming into the Dip. Finally he just let her go and she took off with a dramatic burst of acceleration. The jockey was committed. He had to let her continue her run, but so spectacular had been the burst that even as she tired coming up the hill, it was clear that she was going to hold the fast-finishing Rosalba. The official distance was a length. Lester Piggott, seated comfortably but impotently on Collyria, had seen all he wanted to see of the wonder filly. Next time out, *he* would have that ride.

Doug Smith later admitted that he had 'kidded' his way on board. On her final work-out on the gallops at Newmarket, he had sensed the grey's huge potential, but he kept his counsel. Lester, on Collyria, had no inkling of the power at the champion jockey's disposal.

'I had ridden her in her final gallop,' said Smith, 'and had formed the opinion that she was a really high class filly. Fortunately, Lester did not ride her in the same gallop and failed to realize just how good she was.' He was not prepared, however, for her fantastic acceleration: '. . . once I had begun my run I had to go on.'

Petite Etoile's time in the 1,000 Guineas was almost two seconds faster than that of Taboun in the colts' equivalent. The point was not lost on Piggott or Murless, though the bookmaking fraternity, sceptical of the staying power of such a speed merchant, refused to see her as a runaway Oaks winner.

Doubts about Petite Etoile's stamina would remain to the end of her days, but in the summer of 1959 she had one priceless asset on her side – the weather. From May to October, the sun blazed down from clear blue skies. The going throughout the country was always good to firm and that suited the filly's very light, top-of-the-ground action. Indeed, so firm was the going that some of the best-bred two-year-olds were kept under wraps until late in the autumn.

In the meanwhile, the seemingly imperturbable trainer had clearly fallen in love with his wonder filly. In an article in the *Daily Express*, he waxed lyrical about his charge:

> Here is a woman's face and a woman's character. She has a very nice, well bred nature but if anything upsets her, well then, all hell breaks loose. She knows she's good. She doesn't stand for any other horses eating near her – she insists they stay at a respectful distance. She is the most intelligent animal I have ever known. She misses nothing. She instantly recognizes me a hundred yards away and demands her present of sugar. She also has a wonderful sense of humour. Sometimes in the box I will pick up a stick and raise it to her in fun and she immediately picks up her leg at me. Any owner or trainer would be very, very exceptionally lucky to get the likes of her just once in a lifetime.

But if she was all sweetness and light with Murless, she was less accommodating with strangers. An incident quoted by Murless concerning Prince Aly Khan's stud manager, Cyril Hall, points up the contrast nicely. 'I remember Cyril Hall coming into Warren Place one December Sales and walking into her box. He said, "You're getting a bit fat, old girl!" He pushed his finger into her neck and she turned round like lightning and got hold of the lapels of his coat and lifted him off the ground. Frightened the life out of him!'

Turf historian Roger Mortimer was one of the filly's greatest supporters, but he had a less than romantic view of her nature. In his summary of the 1959 season, he describes Petite Etoile as 'a perfectly proportioned filly with immense power behind the saddle, she seemed to possess only one fault, namely a pair of rather small and not wholly benevolent eyes'.

Her looks, of course, mattered not at all. What the animal was was superfast and she would prove in the Oaks to be one of the greatest fillies that ever graced a racecourse. Lester Piggott now had the ride and, despite doubts about her stamina, she went to the post at Epsom carrying a great deal of professional as well as public money. Cantelo, a filly out of Chanteur II that had won the Royal Lodge Stakes and later the Cheshire Oaks, was a warm favourite at 7/4, while Lingfield Trial winner Mirnaya was also heavily backed at 2/1. Petite Etoile was marked down to 11/2.

In the event, she won as she liked, going away by three lengths with that blistering turn of foot inside the final half-furlong, Piggott having held her up just in case there wasn't quite enough petrol .in the tank. Cantelo was second with Rose of Medina a further five lengths away third.

It was a marvellous moment for Lester who knew he was sitting aboard the most exceptional filly he had ever ridden. Her acceleration had left the beaten jockeys totally bewildered. Harry Carr, who a couple of days earlier had been bemoaning his fate in the Derby, now said: 'I was level with Lester coming down the hill – but he was only cantering while I was hard at work.' And Eddie Hide added: 'I thought I should outstay the others but just over a furlong out I took a peep behind me and there was Lester Piggott, cantering on Petite Etoile. I still hoped she might not stay and kept my filly going as hard as I could, but Lester went by me easily and the race was over.'

Prince Aly Khan, perhaps swept up by the emotion of the occasion, chided the press for their lack of faith in his animal's stamina. 'You have been too categorical about Petite Etoile,' he said. 'Because she is by Petition and there is fast blood in her pedigree, you set her down only as a miler. But she stayed every yard of the 12 furlongs today and I think she would have stayed *two miles* on this going!'

The superfast ground had certainly helped, but whether Petite Etoile was at the limit of her resources no one was then prepared to say, least of all the celebrating jockey and trainer. It would be many years later that Murless would admit: 'Petite Etoile never got a yard over a mile and a quarter.' And that is what made Lester Piggott's handling of her, and success in the big races, all the more remarkable.

There were to be three more outings that year: the Sussex Stakes at Goodwood, the Yorkshire Oaks and, finally, the Champion Stakes at Newmarket. Such was the filly's reputation that only two other runners contested the Newmarket engagement, and Lester Piggott, as Roger Mortimer put it, 'achieved the not inconsiderable feat of getting her tightly boxed in a field of three. It looked as if she was going to be beaten but close to home a very narrow gap appeared and Piggott squeezed her through to win by half a length leaving one or two punters, who had chosen to lay the odds, in a condition of almost total collapse.'

What happened was vividly described by James Lawton.

In the final furlong it seemed that Piggott was coolly aiming to send Petite Etoile through a slender gap between her rivals Barclay and Javelot. Barclay's rider, Garnie Bougoure, was startled more than he should have been by the dawning awareness of what Piggott was about to do. But he kept his nerve and quite legally closed off the daylight between himself and Javelot, who was ridden by Freddy Palmer. Piggott never faltered. He drove for the rails, despite the fact that Javelot appeared to block any progress other than ground-to-air work, which so far Piggott had not attempted.

Some of the crowd gasped. Some, those whose money was riding with Piggott, groaned. It seemed that Piggott had ridden himself into the blindest of alleys. He could only ride through Javelot, which was physically difficult and legally questionable, certainly with a record like his. Then something happened. Palmer's efforts to maintain Javelot's rhythm suddenly faltered, Javelot's hindquarters swung outwards and there on the rail was a glimmer of light. Piggott hurled Petite Etoile at the gap and beneath him was that magical stirring, that sudden speed which carries horse-racing into a new level of experience. . .

Murless and Cyril Hall, who had earlier pleaded specifically for the jockey to 'go easy on the anxiety today, please', were torn between irritation and euphoria for what they had just witnessed. Palmer was left shaking his head and asking the unanswerable question, 'How could Lester Piggott have done such a thing? It doesn't seem possible.'

And Lester? 'I could still have run round the other side and won.'

The confidence of a great horseman or the arrogance of one unwilling to admit he might, just might, have made a mistake? There were many takers for the second view, notably Roger Mortimer who stated that Piggott had been 'over confident'. He wasn't the first, but he would by no means be the last to make that accusation.

But still, the result was in the book. No one else could have unravelled so intricate a knot while travelling at 40 miles an hour. The racing public were seeing the full flowering of a genius that summer and it was quite appropriate that, as Britain went to the polls in the autumn to elect a new government, the slogan that screamed out from every tree, every hoarding, was 'YOU'VE NEVER HAD IT SO GOOD'.

It was certainly true of Lester Piggott.

8 St Paddy

As the drab, austere fifties finally loosed their stranglehold on the nation, a burst of energy and optimism swept the land. Suddenly, everything seemed possible. It was time to make great plans for the future.

Lester had done just that. He'd decided he wanted to be champion jockey, win a third Derby and get married. Especially, he wanted to get married. For over a year he had been dating the pretty, brunette daughter of Newmarket trainer Sam Armstrong. Susan, slim, intelligent and with a sparkling sense of humour, was as much in love with the horse-racing world as Lester, and their shared interest gave them a firm base on which to explore other facets of their personalities. It was an ideal match.

Despite their ties with Newmarket, it was decided that a wedding in the town would be impractical. It could quickly turn into a media jamboree and no doubt the whole population would want to be present. So, instead, the elegant grandeur of St Mark's church in London's North Audley Street was chosen. There were thirty-three guests. Afterwards, Lester in a blue pin-striped suit with padded shoulders and Susan in a simple beige dress went on to Brown's Hotel for a champagne and caviar reception. Telegrams of congratulations filled every available space. There simply wasn't time for the best man, assistant trainer John Sutcliffe, to read them all, so the couple departed for a honeymoon in Nice with plenty of reading material for the plane.

The Armstrongs' gift to their new son-in-law and his bride was a television set and furniture for their new home. Susan and Lester exchanged desks, a practical choice if ever there was one. Both would become centres of operation in the Piggott household in the years to come, always littered with form books, address books and the diaries in which Lester enters his bookings.

When Lester returned to Warren Place, it was to find that the big colt St Paddy, bred by Sir Victor Sassoon and on whom Murless was pinning his 1960 classic hopes, was still very backward, and training gallops convinced them both that the 2,000 Guineas would probably come too soon.

But the colt was hard to predict and Murless decided to run him in what looked a moderate field. Sure enough, St Paddy wasn't ready and he finished sixth after showing well for three-quarters of a mile. The winner was Martial, ridden by a newcomer to the British racing scene, 32-year-old Australian Ron Hutchinson. It was Hutchinson's first sight of the famous Rowley Mile and he rode Newmarket like a veteran to land the odds for Irish trainer Paddy Prendergast.

Piggott and St Paddy were reunited for the Dante Stakes over Lester's favourite race course, York, on 18 May, and this time they won in a canter. Lester's report was full of optimism, and indeed plans seemed to be shaping well for the season. Petite Etoile, still in training as a four-year-old, had won first time out in the Victor Wild Stakes at Kempton Park and was well on target for Epsom's Coronation Cup. But there was a pall of gloom over the stables, despite all the success.

Five days after seeing Petite Etoile win, Prince Aly Khan was dead, killed outright in a car smash on the Bois de Boulogne in Paris. It was a shattering blow, not just to the trainer but to the racing world in general. In 1959, Aly Khan's horses had won the 2,000 Guineas, the 1,000 Guineas, the Oaks, the Champion Stakes and the Middle Park Stakes to set a new English record of over £100,000 in winnings. In France he had done equally well, capturing the Arc and the 1,000 Guineas. At the time of his death, he owned six stud farms in Ireland, four in France and over 100 brood mares.

The 1960 Derby received the biggest build-up in newspaper history. It was to be the first televised Derby and the BBC, who had the exclusive rights, made a meal of it. The fairs and the fashion shows, the gypsies and the jugglers, became TV fodder as the cameras roamed the downs in search of the unusual and the bizarre.

St Paddy's York performance had receded in significance in the weeks before the big race. The quality of the opposition now came in for serious scrutiny and the racing press concluded that St Paddy was a possibility rather than a probability. The one they all seemed to like was the French-trained Angers, winner of the Prix Hocquart at Longchamp over the Derby distance the previous month. Angers had a long, ground-devouring stride and seemed to gallop his opponents into the ground. But at least one critic had noticed a chink in the French colt's action and plumped firmly for St Paddy.

As the tapes went up on the seventeen runners, Die Hard, son of Lester's 1954 winner, Never Say Die, shot to the front with Auroy and the well-fancied Marengo just behind. Piggott on St Paddy and Scobie Breasley on Alcaeus had covered the break, but they need hardly have worried because suddenly the pace dropped so dramatically that they seemed to be cantering. This suited Lester fine because he knew his animal had a turn of foot, whereas Angers needed to be hard ridden throughout.

At the mile post, Tudor Period took them on with Port St Anne, Die Hard, Oak Ridge and Marengo heading St Padding and Auroy. Then they were running down the hill towards Tattenham Corner and Lester moved St Paddy on to the rails in third place, still sitting like a statue on the big colt's back.

Into the straight with a quarter of a mile to go, Die Hard began to blow hard and with the field coming back to him Lester decided it was time to go. As he allowed St Paddy to quicken, he was a puzzled man. He had been expecting to hear the pounding hooves of Angers challenging him out of Tattenham Corner, but there was no sign of the French favourite, and as the winning post grew in his sights, he realized there wasn't going to be. He had the race in his pocket.

St Paddy flashed across the line three lengths clear of the improving Alcaeus, with Kythnos half a length away third. It was a textbook ride for the 24-year-old who had now completed two legs of his personal treble. Now he would be going all out for that champion jockey title.

After the race, Lester was barely out of breath as he told reporters, 'It was my easiest win yet. I was always in the first six and coming down the hill was lying about fifth behind Port St Anne and Tudor Period, who were making the running. I moved up into third at Tattenham Corner and just over two furlongs out went past Die Hard. There was never any question of those behind me catching St Paddy. It was certainly the easiest of all my Derby wins.' Lester went off to weigh in impervious to the muted, almost sombre mood in the unsaddling enclosure. He had not yet heard the word that stunned Epsom and now hung like a pall over the downs. Angers had been shot.

'As the horse ran down the hill, I heard a terrible click,' said a tearful Georges Thiboeuf, Angers' jockey. 'The horse seemed to sink before me. I knew then he had broken a fetlock, but when I saw the leg I felt as though I was going to be ill.' Vet John Garrett, who was following the runners in a car, said, 'There was no hope of saving the horse and I had to shoot him quickly. His leg was broken in several places and the animal was in a bad way.'

The tragedy quickly took on a human dimension when the animal's owner, Mrs Ralph Strassburger, was told of the colt's death. She was distraught. Winning the Derby had been the thirty-year ambition of her husband Ralph, who had died the previous year, and it was in his memory that she had kept Angers in training. A week before the race, a £200,000 bid for the colt from bookmaker William Hill had been turned down.

In 1960 Derby quickly became dubbed the Hoodoo Derby in the popular press. Angers had not been the only casualty. On the Tuesday before the race, a fancied Irish outsider, Exchange Student, broke a leg while working on the course and had to be destroyed, while shortly before the animals had gone to the post, Vienna, Sir Winston Churchill's lively contender, was pricked by a nail while being shoed and was forced to withdraw, carrying a mountain of sentimental money for the Grand Old Man of British politics.

But all these sad facts were of no concern to the jockey who had notched up yet another milestone in history. He couldn't afford them to be. The Coronation Cup beckoned and, with it, another ride on the peerless Petite Etoile who had been trained to the minute by Murless for this highlight of its four-year-old campaign.

This time, there were to be no repeats of Lester's heart-stopping antics in the Champion Stakes. It was again a three-horse race but one of the three was Parthia, the popular 1959 Derby winner, ridden by Harry Carr. Lester was always well placed and he hardly needed to touch the accelerator as the remarkable filly cruised home in the final 100 yards. It had been quite a week.

Petite Etoile had held her form so well that Murless decided she should go for the big prize of the King George VI and Queen Elizabeth Stakes at Royal Ascot, but he was aware of how much work she would need to do at home if she was to come to the race fully tuned up. As a rule of thumb, fillies tend to lose form quickly as four-year-olds. In Murless's view, 'You've got to string mares up if you are going to keep them and they are going to take on the colts. I think it is against the run of nature.' But Petite Etoile was an exception, and Murless had a secondary reason for keeping her going – to impress the late Aly Khan's heir, the new Aga Khan, who had inherited a racing empire but had as yet no great love for the sport.

Lester appreciated the point. He was as anxious as Murless that the Aly Khan horses should remain in training instead of being sold off in a massive jumble sale. There were plenty of potential winners still in the pack. He knew, too, that barring accidents or some other unforeseen circumstances, Petite Etoile ought to trot up in the King George. There was no reason to change riding tactics when an animal had such a burst of speed.

But unforeseen circumstances were to come raining down on the Warren Place duo, first quite literally, in the shape of torrential rain which soaked the ground and made the going extremely heavy, and secondly in the persons of Scobie Breasley and Jimmy Lindley, who in quite separate ways rode the races of their lives.

Scobie Breasley was harbouring a grudge. In his biography, he tells of an incident at Wolverhampton when Piggott, he alleges, tried to put him over the rails. The pair were out-and-out rivals for the jockeys' championship in 1960 so it is reasonable to suppose that there was plenty of friction between the two in the nail-biting rush for the title. But whether or not you believe that Lester did indeed cut up his rival so dangerously, it is easy enough to believe Breasley's planned revenge at Ascot.

'My first reaction,' he says, after the Wolverhampton incident, 'was to give Lester a smack on the nose but the only way to get back at him that made any sense was to hit him where it would hurt most – in his pocket. Getting involved in a fight could have cost me my licence so I would have finished worse off.' So Breasley concocted a more subtle way of getting his own back.

'Petite Etoile was *the* horse of the moment,' he says. 'She was going to be a real hot shot for the King George VI and Queen Elizabeth Stakes at Ascot with Lester on her back. That would be the day to teach Lester a lesson. My mount, the Irish colt Sunny Court, had no real chance of winning but I decided to do my level best to stop Lester collecting the big prize. I didn't intend to break the rules but I was determined to give Lester a hard time and so square the books.'

What Breasley had in mind was to box Piggott in. He was well aware of Lester's preferred habit of reserving his mount for a final furlong sprint and, equally, he was aware that the tactic depended on the jockey contriving a clear run. With Lester on board, it usually worked, but he had shown a degree of over-confidence before – and if he did so this time, it might just prove fatal.

Piggott and Murless, oblivious to Breasley's secret witch-hunt, were concerned only that Petite Etoile might not get the trip. Both were convinced by now that the horse was not a true mile-and-a-half animal but that she could get the trip in the right conditions and ridden the right way. That meant delaying the challenge to conserve stamina.

Parthia was again in the field as well as the five-year-old Aggressor, a real mudlark who had the incomparable Jimmy Lindley on his back. The other danger might come from Kythnos, ridden by the promising Geoff Lewis. It was never going to be as easy as the 2/5 odds on the book suggested. In the event, it was to prove impossible.

Coming into the short straight, Lester had Petite Etoile on the rails – but last – and a quarter of a mile from home she received a hefty bump. Scobie Breasley takes up the story. . .

> By the time Lester had shaken me off and got out of the pocket on the rails, Jimmy Lindley and Aggressor had the race won. I was only sixth but came back grinning like a Cheshire cat. Everyone thought that Lester had ridden a bad race and Jimmy Lindley probably thinks to this day that he and Aggressor stole the King George but that's the real story of how the wonder filly was beaten. In normal circumstances I would have given Lester plenty of room if his mount was going so much better than mine, but this time I kept the door firmly shut. Of course, Lester knew perfectly well what had gone on but, to give him his due, he didn't complain. In fact he never said a word to anyone about what prevented his filly getting a decent run. Lester took it like a man. He's never mentioned it from that day to this – at least not to me – but he never tried to put me over the rails again.

Better judges than I consider Breasley's account somewhat fanciful, Richard Baerlein among them. 'If the ground had been good or normal, Aggressor wouldn't have been in the first three. He loved soft ground and it just came up to suit him. Lester did get boxed in and had to come round on the outside. But Aggressor got first run and if Petite Etoile could have handled the ground, she would still have won the race.'

Murless said later, 'A lot of people blamed Lester, but I never did. In my view he did just the right thing, sticking on the rails, and he might have scraped through. What's more, after that bump he did the only possible thing in coming to the outside.' At the finish Petite Etoile was beaten half a length. The racegoers were stunned. The press was stunned. What went wrong? they chorused. 'I think they cut the grass the wrong way,' said the master of the one-liner. And that, as far as Lester was concerned, was that.

But disappointing though the defeat may have been to the Murless connection, there were still one or two tasty dishes left on the menu that summer. St Paddy was to go for the St Leger.

First, he would have a tune-up at Goodwood and a final prep at York before taking on the cream of the three-year-old crop over Doncaster's one and three-quarter miles. He opened the second half of his summer campaign somewhat miserably, giving 5 lb in the Gordon Stakes on the beautiful Sussex course and finding nothing in the finish when Kipling took him on in the final furlong to stay on by half a length. St Paddy had been 8/11 favourite, but it was clear that he needed the outing as he returned to the enclosure blowing and puffing uncharacteristically from his afternoon's work. Murless was not unduly dismayed, neither was Lester. At York on 17 August he seemed almost back to his best as he captured the Great Voltigeur Stakes from the useful colt Blue Peter. It was enough to establish him as comfortable favourite for the Doncaster test, and had word of his subsequent work on the gallops at Newmarket leaked out, he would have gone to post unbackable.

Murless remembered the final work-out as the most exciting of his whole career. He took on Red Pins, Off Key, Sunny Way, Exar and Primera, giving weight to all of them, and, with Lester on board, left them for dead. He was ready all right.

As the runners – which this time included Sir Winston Churchill's unlucky Derby contender Vienna – paraded in the ring at Doncaster, St Paddy looked trained to perfection. 'Fit to run for his life,' was how Roger Mortimer described him, noting too that Anaram and Die Hard also looked at their very best. Conditions, too, were perfect. The bookmakers, still not entirely convinced of St Paddy's true quality, bearing in mind the Angers tragedy in the Derby, allowed him to start at 4/6, a price which was happily taken by many a canny Yorkshire punter. Their brass was in safe hands.

The field got off first time, but hardly at a gallop. Off Key took them along with Spartan Green, St Paddy and Oak Ridge trailing and Die Hard making his way in the centre of the field. The order remained virtually the same for the first mile and then Spartan Green quickened, taking Off Key and St Paddy with him to the final turn. From the grandstand it was clear that Piggott's colt was simply idling. Vienna and Die Hard were the first to make a race of it, disputing the battling Spartan Green's lead three furlongs from home until Lester Piggott signalled it was time to get serious and nudged St Paddy into his work. A quarter of a mile from home and the contest was effectively over. St Paddy was on the bit, Lester Piggott was looking all around him and the only race still going on was between Vienna, Die Hard and Oak Ridge for the minor placings.

Die Hard got the verdict from Vienna but by the time they passed the finishing post one half expected to see Lester Piggott showered, changed and on his way home. It really was that easy.

It wasn't just Lester's first St Leger. The remarkable Sir Victor Sassoon was also winning a race he had pursued relentlessly since 1927 when Hot Knife finished second to Book Law. In the space of just seven years he had captured four Derbies to add to previous successes in the 2,000 and 1,000 Guineas. Now he had his grand slam. 'I'm over-whelmed,' he said afterwards. 'Many people asked me today whether I was nervous about the result but quite honestly I thought St Paddy would stay the full distance. What made me so confident was pure coincidence. When he won the Derby, St Paddy was No. 20 on the card and it was my brother-in-law's twentieth wedding anniversary. When he won the Voltigeur it was my wife's birthday and today, of all things, it is my brother-in-law's birthday.' In racing, you seek your omens where you will.

Lester was self-effacing almost to the point of embarrass-ment. There simply wasn't a story of the race to tell. 'He was never really off the bit,' he told the earnest men with their open notebooks. 'He was always in a canter. It was a nice, even pace and I couldn't help going to the front.' Not exactly red-blooded headline stuff, but it had to do. *The Times* summed it up next day: 'ST PADDY CANTERS AWAY WITH THE ST LEGER'.

And Lester Piggott, two classics tucked under his belt, also cantered away with the champion jockey's title. His total of 170 winners eclipsed his previous best by a comfortable margin and, more importantly, eclipsed his great rival Scobie Breasley. 1960 had delivered all Lester had asked for and done rather well by Noel Murless too, who became champion trainer for the second successive time. Forty-two races had been won, £118,297 had been trawled into the coffers for his owners. The new Aga Khan had decided he liked this racing game and would keep his father's racing empire intact. And sitting happily in the stables back at Warren Place was an unraced two-year-old named Pinturischio who might – just might – be better than all those worthy champions who had gone before him.

The new decade was all set to be a scorcher.

9 | *Pinturischio*

'I've had enough bad luck with that horse. I think we'd be well advised to change his name before we run him in the Eclipse and the St Leger . . . ' The speaker was Sir Victor Sassoon, dolefully digesting the news that had just reached him at home in the Bahamas – Pinturischio was out of the 1961 Derby.

The wonder colt had been doped, nobbled by a gang so ruthless and determined, that three weeks after a first attempt had been thwarted by the animal's own powers of recovery, they had returned to Warren Place and coolly doped him again. The second attempt nearly killed him. And it killed, too, the hopes of thousands of punters who had laid a fortune on the horse in the ante-post market. 'He would have won it all right,' said a blazing Lester Piggott. 'People who dope horses should be shot.'

It was Pinturischio's astonishing reputation that had brought about his downfall. Before he'd even been seen on a racecourse, much less run on one, he had been backed down to 4/1 for the 2,000 Guineas and 5/1 for the Derby. Bookmakers called him 'The Talking Horse' because of all the money bet solely on the basis of rumour – informed rumour, it must be added, because the Watchers on the Heath rarely get it wrong. But, even so, William Hill's spokesman described as 'quite fantastic' the £20,000 and £15,000 his firm received in ante-post bets with one punter laying £2,000 to £10,000 for the Newmarket classic.

With that kind of money sloshing around, the temptations were obvious and doping had become a national scandal in the fifties and early sixties before improved security and more precise forms of chemical analysis turned it back into a high-risk business for the ungodly. Warren Place was one of the most secure stables in the land. Even so, the gang had got to Pinturischio without even getting their knees dirty. In Tim Fitzgeorge Parker's biography of Murless, the trainer described what happened.

> I was warned a few days beforehand that he would be nobbled, but I didn't think that anything would happen until the horse had run in the Dante Stakes at York on May 16 [the Derby was due to be run on May 31]. Later, some woman wrote an article in one of the Sunday papers saying that they had sat up in the big tree at the back of the yard and waited until everything was closed up for the night and then got in through the skylight of Pinturischio's box. Of course they did not get in through the skylight. They just picked the locks on the door. Then they gave him a very strong physic, the stuff, I believe, that they give to elephants. It must have been terribly powerful. He was never the same horse again and although for a short while I hoped that I would be able to get him right to run in the Derby, they broke in a second time and made no mistake. They really finished him off. In fact, from their point of view, they did such a good job that he was never able to run again.

It was Lester Piggott who discovered him the first time. 'I went to his box to do work and found him helpless,' he recalled. Both Piggott and Murless knew immediately what had happened, but while the trainer tried to work a miracle, it was decided to say nothing. Warren Place went about its normal, bustling business despite the battery of long-range press cameras that recorded every move, both in the stables and on the gallops. The tension in the next few days was palpable but Murless kept his nerve, and after a little over a week, it seemed the crisis might be over.

It was not. Pinturischio's recovery might not have been complete but the risk was too great for the Mister Big whose money was riding sweatily on the outcome. On the evening of 26 May, he sent in the gang again, and that was that.

Apart from the punters who had lost a collective fortune, Lester Piggott had lost his Derby mount. It added heat to his anger because he had never for a moment doubted that the colt would cruise home at Epsom. 'Everything he did at home suggested he would win,' he said, adding of Pinturischio's disappointing fourth place in the 2,000 Guineas, 'He was a long way short of his best that day.'

With the betting market now in turmoil, the French colt Moutiers was installed as Derby favourite, but the firm ground was all against him and the 5/1 chance could manage no better than fourteenth. The winner was Psidium at 66/1, a price that had frightened off all but soothsayers, and possibly relatives of his owner, a Mrs Arpad Plesch. The silence that greeted him in the winner's enclosure was positively deafening, and embarrassing for his highly regarded trainer, Harry Wragg. But there it was, and as for Lester, he had watched the whole grisly episode at home on TV.

But better days were ahead. In fact, they had already begun with the birth of Lester's first child at the beginning of May. The birth was two weeks late and in the final few days before Susan finally delivered, Lester became notably restive and edgy. It was reflected in his riding which seemed more daring than ever – if that's possible – and at Chester on 4 May he was up before the stewards no less than three times in the same afternoon.

The advent of the camera patrol had done much to tighten up discipline on the race track and justice off it. Not every course had one, but Chester had made the investment and now Lester found himself watching sheepishly along with fellow jockeys Scobie Breasley and Harry Carr as the stewards screened the closing stages of the Grosvenor Stakes. Lester, on the favourite Pre-emptive, was shown driving his mount towards an almost non-existent gap which, after a little bumping and boring, firmly closed. Lester found himself beaten into fourth place behind Half Moon and asked to explain his riding. His punishment was a caution, a great improvement on the days when every steward in the land was said to be gunning for him. No action was taken on his riding of Chrysler III in the Chester Cup when he appeared to get into difficulties on the tight final bend.

Not exactly another ho-hum day at the office, then. And when he finally arrived wearily back at his hotel it was to take a telephone call from the hospital. It was Susan. 'Lester, it's a girl!' she declared triumphantly. He was thrilled, even if it did mean forking out a fiver to a fellow jockey after betting it would be a boy. In fact the promptness with which the fiver was paid became the talking point of jockeys' changing rooms for weeks.

The disappointment of Pinturischio and the Derby was quickly put behind him when Lester and Petite Etoile, now in a matronly fifth year, 'stole' the Coronation Cup from Sir Winston Churchill's colt Vienna. Coming into the home straight, Vienna headed Proud Chieftain with Lester in third, sitting still as a statue on Petite Etoile. Inside the final furlong, Vienna and Proud Chieftain were locked in a grim, heaving struggle. Lester just glided up on their outside and Petite Etoile, still hard held, merely stuck out a winning neck as they cruised over the line. It was Lester's cheekiest bit of riding yet.

Petite Etoile was to lose one and win one before one of the great partnerships in racing came finally to a close, but meanwhile, Lester had turned his attention to the giant colt Aurelius which, after a backward start, was now beginning to look like St Leger material.

Aurelius was Pinturischio's working partner at Warren Place and it had been the horse's emphatic Craven Stakes victory in April, hard ridden by Lester Piggott, that had sent Pinturischio's price tumbling for the classics. All those who had seen the two together in the training gallops rated Pinturischio at least a stone better than his stable companion. So, if Aurelius was that good, ran the argument, Pinturischio must be phenomenal. It is easy to see how such a thread of logic can became a veritable hawser of conviction in something as combustible as the betting market.

As a yearling, Aurelius was so big that many potential purchasers felt he would be impossible to train. Noel Murless demurred. 'Difficult, not impossible' was his verdict, and he promptly snapped up the colt for a bargain-basement price of 5,000 guineas. It proved a marvellous investment. As well as opening his three-year-old career with that Craven Stakes win, Aurelius also landed big prizes at Ascot and Sandown, so that by the time he came to the St Leger, he had more than paid his way.

It was generally felt that the St Leger field was sub-standard in 1961. Just Great, emphatic winner of the traditional St Leger prep, the Great Voltigeur Stakes, was warmly regarded, though, and so was the French colt Dicta Drake. Lester felt he had a chance on Aurelius but would put it no higher than that. As it turned out, all the cards were thrown into his lap.

As the horses lined up for the start, Pinzon, drawn number one next to the rails, refused to go into his right position. The starter had an otherwise faultless line and was anxious to get the field away. Pinzon's jockey Ed Larkin took the hint and switched his mount to the other side of Sempervivum (drawn 2) leaving Scobie Breasley to fill the gap on the rails. It seemed a sensible arrangement. But as the tapes went up, both Pinzon and Sempervivum jinked across Just Great causing the animal to rear right up on his hind legs. He seemed suspended for ever as Scobie fought just to stay in the saddle, and when he finally did come back to earth, he promptly wheeled to the right before turning to face the course. By now the last train was long gone and the disgusted Australian was left with the humiliating alternative of cantering the St Leger second favourite one and three-quarter miles around the Doncaster countryside.

So that was the first bit of luck for Lester, although he was completely unaware of it. The second came when the pacemaker Noel Murless had put into the race, Hunter's Song, fooled the inexperienced French jockey Max Garcia into taking too early a lead.

Eph Smith, following orders to the letter, had set just the pace Murless and Piggott wanted for Aurelius. When Hunter's Song ran out of steam, three-quarters of a mile from home, he dropped back quickly, leaving the startled Garcia way out on his own. Lester began tracking him, feeding off the Frenchman's pace, slowly reeling him in like a fish on a line. Inside the final two furlongs, Dicta Drake was finished. He had nothing left to resist Lester's smooth challenge on Aurelius and the Piggott–Murless combination crossed the line three-quarters of a length to the good.

'I felt confident about beating Dicta Drake after seeing that he was at full stretch,' said Lester, 'but coming up the straight, I was worrying about when Scobie would come at me.' He was unaware of the scrimmage at the start. Actually, Lester was nearly caught on the run-in by local boy Joe Sime on Bounteous, who finished like an express. Murless, though pleased to have landed another classic, was quick to put the race into perspective when he said, 'This was not a vintage St Leger. Aurelius is not in the Crepello or St Paddy class but he is better than Ridge Wood, my 1949 winner. Aurelius would never have won today if he had run in the Derby,' he added. 'He would have been stumped up.'

So, in the end, Lester was able to reflect on a highly satisfactory season despite losing his champion jockey title to arch-rival Scobie Breasley. There hadn't been much in it, just half a dozen winners or so with Lester finishing on the 164 mark, his second best to date. Noel Murless had carried off the top trainer's title for the third year in a row and the £95,972 he brought in meant that everyone connected with Warren Place was doing very nicely thank you. Certainly Lester had no complaints, and his frequent sorties abroad had also netted him a tidy sum to count for the winter.

This new-found wealth, however, was not reflected particularly in his life-style. There was a fast and extremely handsome car in the driveway of his Newmarket home, but it was soon to become the province of a chauffeur after Lester's persistent speeding earned him a six-month ban. By the mid-sixties he had managed to rack up ten convictions for motoring offences. None of which seemed to bother him much. In fact, he treated his brushes with the law with a tolerant good humour, once giving his name laughingly as John Brown after being stopped for taking a short cut down a one-way street in Newmarket.

Perhaps the biggest change connected with Lester came in his riding style, which was subtle enough to be overlooked but later would become utterly distinctive. He had begun to shorten his stirrup leathers in the manner of leading French jockey, Yves St Martin. He found it gave him a better point of balance over the horse and while it left him slightly vulnerable to an animal that might shy in the parade ring or at the start, it was a great advantage in a driving finish. Nowadays, so many jockeys have copied the style that it has become virtually the norm. But it never was a style suited to everyone and critics of the trend have grown more vocal in their opposition in recent seasons.

One thing that didn't change in 1961 was Lester's all-out determination and ability to ride a strong finish. His use of the whip had become another talking point and although he did appear to rely heavily on the instrument, he didn't always use it. Sometimes a lazy horse will need a sharp reminder; sometimes just a sight of the whip will be enough to galvanize it into action. Lester used both methods to equal effect in his all-action finish.

Considering his reputation for chasing winners to the point of recklessness, it was supremely ironic that 1962 should begin with Piggott being accused, and banned, for 'not trying'. It was a case which rocked the racing world and left a residue of bitterness far more potent than the rough riding ban of 1954.

Staffordshire trainer Bob Ward had two horses, Ione and Polly Macaw, entered in a selling race at Lincoln. He had engaged Lester for whichever of the two rides he preferred, although stressing that Polly Macaw was by far the better of the two. Yet Ione was the odds-on favourite and Lester opted for Ione. You can guess what happened next. Polly Macaw ran true to her home form and romped away with the race while Lester, well beaten on Ione, dropped his hands on the run-in to avoid giving Ione too hard a ride. Trainer and rider were immediately summoned before the stewards, their explanations rejected and the case referred to the Jockey Club in London.

The hearing took place on the eve of the Derby, in which Lester was to partner Noel Murless's Young Lochinvar. Before the Jockey Club were to announce their sentence,

Lester was in jovial mood at a Press Club lunch where he
summed up prospects for the race, including his own which
he described as 'a fair each-way chance'. Prospects for his
exoneration on the 'not trying' charge seemed rather better.
He went to Portman Square in a confident mood. He left in a
black fury.

Press and racegoers jostled and pushed to get near the jockey as he ran out of the front door and into a waiting car. 'I've
been told to say nothing,' he yelled, with the clear implication that he'd like to say plenty, and then he roared off into
the London traffic. So the press turned to Ward who
emerged from the building grey and hunched. 'The Jockey
Club told me they are withdrawing my licence,' he told his
shocked audience. 'I am absolutely flabbergasted.' It was
left to senior steward Lord Crathorne to announce Piggott's
fate – a six-week ban.

So, once again, Lester was out of the Derby, and he was
furious. When he returned to his Newmarket home, the press
were out in force and he was in no mood to deal with them.
The *Daily Mail* reported gleefully how he 'landed a crushing
left hook on one reporters' jaw,' and 'hurled stones at the
press as he disappeared into his home'. Dramatic stuff. Lester was living up to form, providing good copy.

The six-week ban seemed more interminable than the
three months with Jack Jarvis. Now all Lester could do was
sit at home and watch as the winners filed past his window or
flickered to life on his television screen. He should have been
out there, riding hell for leather to get his title back; instead,
his season would end with a meagre 96 winners from 458
rides and no classic success.

In a sense there was consolation in that, for Young
Lochinvar proved to be as inept as its rivals over the Epsom
gradients in a race which saw seven brought down and the
winner emerge as a 22/1 shot called Larkspur. His trainer
was one M. V. O'Brien, a name that would reappear from
time to time in the classic annals!

It would be fanciful to describe 1962 as a signal for a slump
in the upward graph of Piggott's progress, but there was a
levelling off. And the same was true of the Murless stable

where the master trainer was forced to give best first to Dick Hern and then to Ireland's Paddy Prendergast. The winners still came in, so did the money. But they weren't classic winners – and there were none on the horizon.

Lester has never made any secret of his insatiable appetite for riding (and winning) classics. His pursuit of Frank Buckle's record was as resolute as it was inexorable. So when the supply line began to dry up a little at Warren Place, it was natural that he should begin to wonder whether he was still the right man in the right place, or whether some new phase in his career should be explored. In 1963-4 it was something he couldn't quite put into words, or even identify. But when towards the end of a sensationally successful 1965 season (champion but again no classic) he began to cast his eye around, he saw plenty of trainers with strong hands to play in the classic game – and most had their eyes on him.

10 | *Riding Out Alone*

The line from Tipperary was not a good one, but above the wheezing and the whistling Lester could just make out the soft Irish tones of Vincent O'Brien and the name he kept repeating, V-A-L-O-R-I-S. O'Brien didn't need to spell it out, Lester could have picked up the name by telepathy. The Irish 1,000 Guineas champion was one of the hottest properties in racing, especially since an outbreak of swamp fever on the other side of the Channel had resulted in a temporary ban on French horses.

'Would you like to ride her? In the Oaks?' asked O'Brien.

'Of course I'll ride her,' said Lester, and so kicked away the last plank from under him.

The Fall of the House of Piggott and Murless rocked the racing world in a way no doping or betting scandal could ever do, The public was outraged. In eleven tearaway seasons, the Warren Place duo had annexed seven English classics, four champion jockey titles and well over three-quarters of a million pounds in prize money. It was a team. *The* team. To break it up was unthinkable – and for what? A filly who might – only might – add a single notch to the Piggott totem of classics? The emotional temperature ran so high the mercury was bubbling.

Of course, it was never that simple. The relationship between the two men had been under strain for some time and communications must have been at a very low ebb indeed for Murless to be so jolted by the Valoris affair. But the press were happy to fuel the image of Murless – calm, dignified, stoical – as the severely injured party. There was no serious attempt to explore the background to the story, and the specific facts that led Piggott to Valoris were never reported at the time.

Varinia was the Warren Place stable's best hope for the 1966 Oaks, though her two-year-old form had been patchy. Her first serious examination would be the Oaks Trial at Lingfield Park and it was only natural that Murless would put Piggott up for this vital tune-up race. But Lester begged off. The Oaks Trial clashed with the big race at Ayr on 14 May, and Lester, having partnered the great stayer Aegean Blue to victory in the Chester Cup, now had a chance to partner the tough colt again. So, instead, Murless turned to another stable jockey, Stan Clayton, to ride Varinia and the new combination duly trotted in. So did Lester, breaking the Ayr course record. And later that weekend he dropped the hint that he might not be on Varinia in the Oaks.

The press naturally pounced. Murless found himself under siege to explain this surprising change of riding plans, and the answer he was forced to give didn't please him at all. Lester had said in effect, 'Stan Clayton won on her in the Trial, he can ride her in the Oaks.' As the jockey said later, 'Noel seemed to take it for granted that I was still stable jockey and that I would automatically ride his filly at Epsom. Like all the top English trainers Noel had always been accustomed to having his stable jockey riding the horses both in their home work and on the racecourse. The whole thing was a shock to him. It upset all his arrangements and disturbed his way of life. The papers, of course, made a sensation of it.'

And sensation nearly followed on the racecourse when Piggott and Valoris were finally united for the big race. The Irish filly shied so badly after leaving the parade ring that Lester was almost unshipped. As he later noted with heavy irony, 'It would have delighted my many critics at the time if I had been parted from Valoris before the race. I wonder how many officials would have bothered to catch her!' The jockey had felt the hot breath of hostility on his neck everywhere he moved at Epsom, but if it troubled him, he didn't show it. Instead, consummate professional that he is, he took Valoris quietly back to the paddock, dismounted and led her all the way through the crowds, down the hill and up the other side to the start. By the time they got to the stalls, the filly was totally calm and composed.

Whatever else the public thought of Lester, they had reason to be grateful for his careful nursing of their investment. Valoris started at 11/10 while Varinia was no better than 100/7 on the book. Still, Stan Clayton seemed determined to make a nonsense of the odds as he jumped Varinia off at the start and set a fierce pace up the hill to the mile post. The filly's stamina was well known, but Valoris was proving she too had staying power, and coming down Tattenham Hill Lester had his mount nicely tucked in fourth. When he let her go, one and a half furlongs from the finish, Lester knew his ninth classic was in the bag.

Clayton battled on gamely on Varinia but there was never the remotest chance of catching Valoris. The distance between the two rivals was five and a half lengths with Berkeley Springs and Geoff Lewis slipping in between them in the final 150 yards. Noel Murless was disappointed but realistic enough to admit that the presence of Piggott on her back would not have turned Varinia into a winner.

And so began the Phoney War. Piggott had proved his point on Valoris, but where did he go now? Not back to Warren Place. And ominously, there was a genuine danger of some trainers following the strident lead given by Ireland's Paddy Prendergast when he declared in the press, 'I would never engage Lester Piggott again under any terms. Not for the crown jewels of England.' It was a time for cool heads and wise counsel, and fortunately both prevailed.

Peace broke out on 13 July. Murless booked Piggott to ride Pink Gem for his new owner, Jim Joel, in a modest maiden stakes at Newmarket. The champion jockey duly obliged and another £495 found its way into the petty cash tin. But the real significance of the occasion was the occasion itself, and having proved publicly that they weren't about to scratch each other's eyes out, Murless and Piggott were free to concentrate on business again. That meant Royal Ascot, where all the prizes come gilt-edged.

Lester was hardly likely to come up with another eight-timer as he had in 1965, but he still proved he was the master of the beautiful Berkshire course by steering home five winners including Aunt Edith in the King George VI and Queen Elizabeth Stakes. Murless was delighted. The £30,000 prize money was rich compensation for his classic disappointments, and even that barren run might soon be over if the performance of his two-year-old filly Fleet in winning the Princess Maiden Stakes was anything to go by. There was also the unraced Royal Palace sitting at home. Lester would surely relish that one.

Ironically enough, he didn't. The one animal that many believe might have kept him at Warren Place for at least another year gave him no pleasure at all when given a serious examination in the one-mile Royal Lodge Stakes in the Ascot September meeting. Previous outings had shown that Royal Palace was very green but possessed a sharp turn of foot. Just how sharp became evident when Lester brought him from last to first around the outside of the field on the final bend.

Years later, Lester's father Keith was to reveal to Claude Duval just what it was about Royal Palace that turned him off. 'He hasn't got enough guts,' Lester had said when it was suggested he'd been aboard the 1967 Derby winner. Well, only the jockey knows what kind of feel a horse gives him and it may be that Lester sensed some missing chemistry between himself and Royal Palace. Whatever it was, it did nothing to alter the champion's plans. When the season finally ended with Lester again champion jockey with a best-ever tally of 191 winners, he quietly confirmed to Noel Murless his decision to go freelance in 1967.

And that truly was that. The gates of Warren Place clanged shut as far as big-time classic rides were concerned. The partnership was officially over. Dissolved. Others would reap the benefit of Murless's meticulous preparation and fruitful supply line while Lester Piggott the hunter must go and forage on his own.

After the initial shock of the Valoris incident, Murless had been quick to realize just how much he had taken Piggott's presence at Warren Place for granted. He had been complacent and must never get caught short again. So within days of the season ending, he completed a deal with Ayr trainer Harry Whiteman for the transfer of indentures of Sandy Barclay from Cree Lodge to Warren Place. Barclay was widely regarded as a youngster 'in the Piggott mould', and Whiteman even said at the time, 'I'm delighted. Barclay's an absolute genius. I have been in racing for sixty-five years as jockey and trainer and I have never seen anyone like him.'

That took care of the number two spot. Now Murless began to cast around for a jockey worthy of his classic hopefuls, and it was to Australia that he turned his attention.

George Moore was widely regarded as the man of all talents, down under, a wayward genius who could adapt to any conditions, any time, simply because he oozed ability from every pore. Not only was he top dog in Australia but he had also swept all before him in France for the Aly Khan stables. His major European wins included the French Derby and Grand Prix; the Prix de l'Arc de Triomphe and Eclipse Stakes; the Grand Prix de Saint Cloud and the Ascot Gold Cup; the French and Irish 1,000 Guineas; and the Gimcrack and Champion Stakes. There was no doubting the talent – only the temperament.

When Lester heard that George Moore had been approached he was very surprised. The jockey had phoned from Sydney to ask about the lie of the land and the former Murless number one painted a very honest picture of life at Warren Place. Moore was encouraged, Lester nonplussed. What kind of money could Murless be offering? It was widely reported that Moore's Australian earnings topped £25,000 in bonus alone – a huge sum at that time. Piggott couldn't believe he would come.

But come he did and rode a swathe through English racing the like of which no jockey before or since has been able to match. During the height of his powers, Moore would bring home a winner every third ride – a mind-boggling average. And of course he would also take the classics by the scruff of the neck.

By contrast, Lester was to reap the whirlwind, at least initially, when, after a winning start, he was to go thirty-one rides without a winner. Of course, it was small beer compared with the losing sequences other top jockeys have endured; both Steve Donoghue and Doug Smith passed the 120 mark before breaking the spell. But the run was more significant for Lester, feeling his uncertain way in this new freelance world. Finally, it was Noel Murless who enabled him to overcome the drought when he saddled Royal Saint for Piggott at Newbury. It was not, however, a piece of philanthropy on the part of the trainer – the horse's owner, Mrs Vere Hue-Williams, had insisted on 'the best jockey' and that meant Lester Piggott.

From that point onwards the winners began to come in regular enough clusters for Lester to move back into contention for the champion jockey title. At one point, the Australian Ron Hutchinson had gone twenty-six clear and it takes a lot of good horses to peg back that kind of deficit. But if Lester had no other ambition in 1967, it was to retain his crown and stuff the critics' words right back down their throats. The classics, it seemed, would be beyond him.

Already he had watched George Moore bring home Royal Palace and Fleet in the 2,000 and 1,000 Guineas, horses that he might be riding instead of moderate animals like Starry Halo and Royal Saint. And what was to stop Moore repeating the trick in the Oaks and Derby? Not Lester, unless he could conjure some hidden magic out of Fulke Johnson Houghton's Ribocco. The bookmakers didn't think he could and allowed the Ribot-sired colt to bob around in the market at anything from 20/1 to 28/1. Eventually, it went to post at 22/1 while Royal Palace was almost unbackable at 7/4.

This was the Derby of the fleetingly famous El Mighty, a 200/1 no-hoper who became the subject of a much-publicized dream. It's funny how the Derby is prey to so much mumbo-jumbo, far more than its big-betting cousin, the Grand National. You could get lost for days in the jungle of white heather that litters Epsom downs on Derby Day. Anyhow, the Peterborough shopkeeper who'd had the famous dream succeeded in getting El Mighty's price down to as little as 25/1 and, as if to give the mug punters a run for their money, jockey Paul Cook shot the colt from last to first within the opening furlong. After that, common sense prevailed and the race proper began with Royal Palace calling all the shots.

George Moore's confidence seemed justified as he placed Royal Palace in fourth position at Tattenham Corner and then nipped effortlessly into the lead as they entered the straight. But Lester was there too on little Ribocco, bringing his gutsy mount round on the wide outside and then unravelling a solo run in the centre of the course.

As Ribocco drew almost level with the champion coming up to the hill, Moore gave Royal Palace a little reminder and the colt quickened to snuff out the danger within a few strides. As Lester said afterwards, 'I got to him all right but when Moore asked Royal Palace he found an awful lot.' The Australian confirmed that assessment. 'I knew as soon as we met the rising ground he would be all right. Piggott got right up to me on the outside but I hadn't done much by then. I was just waiting for the hill.'

The final distance was two and a half lengths with Dart Board a further two lengths away in third. It gave the Moore–Murless combination its third classic of the season; Fleet failed to make it four two days later when Pia and Eddie Hide captured the Oaks. But it hardly seemed to matter and Royal Palace seemed a certainty to add the St Leger to the tally. 'We will aim for the Triple Crown,' declared a delighted Noel Murless, 'and I expect to run him in the Voltigeur Stakes at York before the St Leger.'

But the best-laid plans . . . Royal Palace did not make the Doncaster engagement. Instead he stayed in his box at Warren Place nursing a badly bruised leg after shying at a workman's drill while exercising at Newmarket and hitting himself hard just above the joint. The news would be a bonus for Lester who again had the ride on Ribocco, and that colt seemed to just get better and better as he went on from Epsom to the Curragh and landed the Irish Sweeps Derby.

Lester has rarely ridden a bad race over the galloping expanse of Ireland's premier race track, and this was no exception. But there were curious factors of which he was unaware working in his favour and they revolved around the man whom the *Daily Mail* was now openly describing as 'the world's greatest jockey', George Moore.

As one stunning victory tumbled over another it seemed that nothing could dent the 43-year-old Australian's super confidence. But something did this day, and it happened not in Ireland but at Cambridge airport where Murless, Moore and the trainer's son-in-law Henry Cecil and his wife Julie Murless were waiting to board a private aircraft. There was a bomb scare which grounded the plane while a search was carried out. The delay had Murless in a quandary, as time was fast running out. And when finally they were allowed to board and taxiing down the runway, a police car suddenly appeared, blue light flashing. 'Go on,' Murless shouted to the pilot and the plane took off with the other passengers wondering idly what all the fuss was about. When the pilot finally told them, Moore was panic-stricken. According to Murless he went white as a sheet and demanded that the pilot turn back at once. The demand was voted down and the plane duly made it across the Irish Sea without mishap. But Moore was a badly rattled man.

'I think that cost us the Sweeps Derby,' Murless recalled in his biography. 'He was in such a state that he shot out far too soon – three furlongs from home – though he was still only beaten half a length.' The incident is recalled with a chuckle, but in the light of events that were to follow, it is easy to forgive Moore for his terror that day. By the end of the season, the papers would be full of the news of the series of threats to Moore and his family that would drive the jockey and his wife and three children to abandon English racing and return to Australia.

Even today, the events are cloaked in mystery, but the threats were real enough, and although neither Moore nor his family were physically harmed, his property certainly was. On one occasion his car was damaged, on another, all his clothing was left shredded after a gang broke into his house. The vendetta was kept secret from the public while the police tried to track down the villains, but they never did, and Moore himself finally revealed what had happened on the eve of his return to Australia.

There seems little doubt that a betting syndicate was responsible. Their goal was 'inside information' and considering Moore was riding a winner every third time in the saddle, it is clear how valuable that information could have been. Jockeys are strictly forbidden to bet or pass on information, but it can and does happen and it is greatly to Moore's credit that he first resisted the blandishments of the villains and then defied their threats. All of which took a heavy toll on a man who was noticeably highly-strung.

At the Curragh, Lester waited patiently for the chance to avenge his Epsom defeat, and perhaps to revise the *Daily Mail*'s opinion as to who was the world's greatest jockey. He knew Ribocco was busting to go but acknowledged that the talent ranged against him was formidable: Scobie Breasley was on Dart Board, one of the genuinely hard-luck Derby stories; the Irish were represented by the fast Royal Sword; and Moore's mount, Sucaryl, was one of the brightest hopes in the Murless stable.

It proved to be a pulsating, dramatic race. Seven furlongs from the finish, Royal Sword suddenly snapped a foreleg and crashed to the turf, catching Breasley on Dart Board a glancing blow as he fell. Somehow, Breasley managed to stay in the saddle, but his chance of winning the race had all but gone. Royal Sword was put down immediately, adding a sad postscript to a race that owed most of its headlines to the Piggott–Moore battle for the prize down the home straight.

As Murless said, the shaken Australian made a dreadful hash of his ride and Sucaryl was pushed to the front fully three furlongs from home. There's nothing Lester likes better than a horse that goes too soon. Feeding off the pace and then pouncing is what he does best, and in the gutsy little Ribocco he had the perfect ally.

Just outside the final furlong, Piggott brought Ribocco up to Sucaryl's heels. Moore could now see as well as hear the danger and his whip rose and fell as he called on his mount for an extra ounce of effort. But, from the grandstand, it was obvious Lester had got him. It was just a matter of when he nudged Ribocco to the front. Inside the final fifty yards, the Great Showman let his animal go and Ribocco was home by a length.

Even allowing for the mistakes and palpable nervousness of Moore, Lester will always be able to look back on this as one of his better races. The full range of his skills were displayed before an Irish crowd that appreciate horsemanship almost as much as a winning bet. Afterwards Lester said in wonder of his mount, 'He was sneaking through openings you wouldn't think a mouse could take.' Small wonder then that Piggott and Ribocco went to Doncaster for the St Leger as joint favourites.

Once again the main opposition would come from Warren Place. Like a conjurer who keeps drawing white rabbits from a top hat, Murless kept saddling outstanding horses. There had never been a year like 1967 for talent at Warren Place; it even eclipsed the Crepello–Petite Etoile era for the sheer depth and range of the animals. Now he was bringing out the Queen's Hopeful Venture, understudy to the absent Derby winner Royal Palace.

For the newspapers, it wasn't just Ribocco v. Hopeful Venture for the Leger, it was also Piggott v. Moore. The rivalry had become as much a part of the season as the superb races it produced. Lester didn't mind one bit. He didn't even bother to deny stories that there was a feud between the two (which there wasn't) because anything that got to 'the other fella' might give Piggott that extra little edge. On such fine points are champions honed.

Ribocco, who after an abysmal start to the season had now got the measure of this big race game, proved to be a more than handy winner at Doncaster. With the sun on his back the little bay responded willingly to every nudge, every instruction from his confident jockey, and while they were slow to leave the starting stalls, Piggott and Ribocco were never under the slightest pressure.

George Moore rode a good race on Hopeful Venture but it was obvious to him that the animal was well below the class of Royal Palace. He said as much after the race, claiming: 'Royal Palace would certainly have won today. No risk. At

his best he is five or six lengths in front of Hopeful Venture.'
Murless agreed. He wasn't unduly perturbed by his failure
to grab a fourth classic, and this time he had no reservations
about the performance of his jockey!

Actually, Moore did well to get Hopeful Venture into second place following a tenacious piece of riding by Claudio
Ferrari on the Italian hope Ruysdael II. Had they not been
locked in such close combat, Scobie Breasley might have
been able to get Dart Board through the gap for a telling run.
As it was, the colt was unlucky for a second time in a classic
race, prompting Breasley to say, 'I'm so sorry for Sir Gordon's [Richards] sake. He had his colt trained to the minute.
I'm sure he would have won.' Lester's reading of the race
rather disputes that: 'Seven furlongs from home I knew I was
going to murder them,' he said.

There were two more races for Piggott and Ribocco, the
Arc de Triomphe and the Washington International. Fulke
Johnson Houghton's colt had already proved itself a veritable fruit machine of a racehorse, spilling out jackpots
whenever Lester pulled the lever, and Charlottown's record
prize money for a season of £101,209 had already been left
more than £20,000 behind.

At Longchamp, there was a near-blanket finish with Bill
Pyers just getting up by a neck on Topyo and Salvo no more
than a short head in front of Ribocco. Race historian Roger
Mortimer later wrote that 'had he enjoyed a trouble-free run
he might just have won'. But even Lester can't keep on picking
up four-leaf clovers. He and Ribocco had had a good run for
their money. And when in Washington the animal clearly
showed the effects of a long season by finishing a distant
ninth behind Fort Marcy it was decided he had had enough.
Shortly afterwards, owner Charles Engelhard announced
that he was retiring the game little colt to stud in Virginia.

And Lester – he retired home to Newmarket to tot up the
profit and loss account of his first freelance season. After a
shaky start, the balance had come up firmly on the credit
side. He was champion jockey for the fourth time in a row
with 117 winners from 557 rides. There were also 100 seconds and 64 thirds, so he was in the frame, one way or

another, every other time he went out to ride. All this had
been achieved with the rides of the country's biggest stable
denied him. He had had to work slavishly, flying and driving
here, there and everywhere in search of a winning ride while
those two brilliant Australians, Scobie Breasley and Ron
Hutchinson, pursued him relentlessly. Hutchinson finally
finished on 111 and Breasley on 109.

Murless, of course, had also had a rather useful season.
He smashed the prize money record with a staggering
£279,775 from 63 winners, and there were three classics into
the bargain. There were so many brilliant three-year-olds
coming out of Warren Place in 1967 that those who have
suggested Lester misjudged the talent at his disposal and
would have stayed with Murless for the sake of, say, Royal
Palace, are well wide of the mark. Lester wanted to go freelance come hell or high water. And if his season had ended in
ruins I have no doubt he would have carried on exactly as
before.

Of course, the opposite happened, and in racing terms at
least, Piggott would never go hungry again. The winds of
change were blowing subtly in favour of the man whom all
but the *Daily Mail* acknowledged as the greatest jockey in the
world. The power base in the classics equation was about to
change as well and other trainers would come forward to
claim the mantle now worn by Noel Murless.

In particular, one Vincent O'Brien of Tipperary would be
heard of more and more. Lester had already established a
good working rapport with the man who had handed him
Valoris. And on his last trip to run the rule over the two-year-
olds at Ballydoyle, Lester had been particularly impressed
by a well-made American-bred colt owned by the American
ambassador to Ireland. Its name was Sir Ivor . . .

11 | *The Year of Sir Ivor*

Sir Ivor was every inch Lester's idea of a classic-winning racehorse, but in the soft, damp spring of 1968 the question was, 'Which kind of classic?' His pedigree posed more questions than it answered.

Sir Ivor had been bred in America, in the bluegrass country of Kentucky, by Mrs Alice Chandler and sent to the Keeneland Sales in July 1966. With a sire like Sir Gaylord, a high-class American miler, and a dam, Attica, that could trace her line back to the Derby record holder Mahmoud, the colt seemed to have the makings of a useful middle-distance horse. But the strain that made doubters of so many came from Royal Charger, an out-and-out sprinter of such class that he once carried top weight to victory in the six-furlong Ayr Gold Cup.

There is, of course, only one thing to do when faced with so much conflicting evidence – try it and see. And that is exactly what breeder Bull Hancock did when he purchased the colt for $42,000 on behalf of Raymond Guest. The animal was immediately booked to go to O'Brien at Ballydoyle, thus re-establishing the partnership that had landed that remarkable Derby win with Larkspur in 1962.

Yet Sir Ivor, for all the quality of his breeding, was no precocious yearling. He had come to Keeneland Sales, 'tall, lanky and lopsided', in the words of his breeder, and because he seemed so backward Hancock and O'Brien agreed to leave him in America to be broken. So it wasn't until

November 1966 that the huge animal touched down on Irish soil. He made an immediate impression on the staff at Ballydoyle, though it wasn't all complimentary. He was so overgrown that no one could visualize him ever racing as a two-year-old. But, not for the first time in his career, Sir Ivor was to confound the critics, and during the early spring of 1967 he began to come on in leaps and bounds. O'Brien was so pleased with progress that he entered him for the six-furlong Tyros Stakes to be run at the Curragh on Irish Derby day, 1 July.

Sir Ivor disappointed. Starting at 3/1 he could manage no better than a close-up fourth, and Liam Ward, his jockey, reported that the animal had really been in need of the race. 'Mind you,' he added, 'the three that finished in front of him today will never do so again.' It was what O'Brien wanted to hear and it was a much fitter and sharper Sir Ivor that went to post on 29 July for the seven-furlong Probationers Stakes. His starting price of 9/4 meant that no fortunes were going to be made and, indeed, he was only once more to start odds against in his whole racing career.

Ward cruised in, just as he had predicted, and O'Brien now began to plan the second half of his two-year-old's campaign with Epsom 1968 a distant but realistic long-term goal. Lester now entered the picture, flying in to Ballydoyle to ride work and being mightly impressed by the range of the young colt. He agreed to ride Sir Ivor in the top French mile race, the Grand Criterium, at Longchamp in October, but meanwhile Ward would give him another spin at the Curragh, this time over seven furlongs in the National Stakes. Again they left the opposition trailing.

Back in England, Lester was also getting to know another classy two-year-old, Petingo, trained by father-in-law Sam Armstrong at Newmarket. The English had yet to see Sir Ivor in the flesh, but what they had seen of Petingo in the Gimcrack Stakes and Middle Park Stakes with Lester aboard had suggested looking no further for the next 2,000 Guineas winner. Armstrong was desperately keen for Piggott to have the ride and when the jockey showed a reluctance to commit himself the trainer realized that O'Brien's animal must indeed be something special. It was going to be a competitive summer.

At Longchamp, Sir Ivor almost literally took the decision out of Piggott's hands. As they approached the two furlong from home marker, trailing the race leader by about six lengths, Lester gave Sir Ivor a nudge. 'He quickened so fast he nearly ran out from under me!' said the astonished jockey afterwards, as Sir Ivor showed for the first time the blistering finishing speed that was to become his hallmark. The French were highly impressed. Sir Ivor had gobbled up their best and done so in a style which brooked no argument.

O'Brien reported to Guest, now American ambassador to Ireland, and suggested that the animal might winter best in a mild climate, away from familiar surroundings. Events have shown that it was such attention to detail in every aspect of a horse's preparation that helped make O'Brien the trainer *par excellence*. Guest was enthusiastic – and confident, too. His belief in O'Brien's genius was total and he was prepared to back that belief in hard cash. Somewhere in the South of France, a well-known bookmaker was holding a betting slip worth £62,500 against Sir Ivor winning the 1968 Derby.

So the cream of the Ballydoyle string were flown to Pisa in November 1967 and settled quickly into the red-tiled training stables close to the famous Leaning Tower. Sir Ivor thrived in the mild climate but, just before Christmas, he developed an abscess in a foot which kept him off the training gallops for fully three weeks. By the time he was ready to be walked again, the colt was bursting with suppressed energy. O'Brien has since revealed how that freshness and the proximity of the stables to a fast-flowing dyke nearly ended the Sir Ivor story at a stroke.

In sheer exuberance, the colt bucked and reared while being walked, and startled rider Johnny Brabston was thrown off. O'Brien, following behind in a car with his head man, rushed to stop the animal escaping and, because Brabston had had the presence of mind to hang on to the reins, they somehow managed to keep the animal from crashing over into the dyke. The memory haunts O'Brien to this day!

There were no further mishaps that winter and by the time Sir Ivor returned to Ballydoyle in the spring he was a very well made animal indeed. He had filled out beautifully and a latent power rippled in every muscle. Yet, curiously enough, he wasn't really ready for the racecourse. His work on the gallops was reported as 'in and out'. Plans to send him to Newmarket for the Gladness Stakes were cancelled and the target was switched instead to Ascot's 2,000 Guineas trial.

Here the ground turned badly against Sir Ivor and it was all Lester could do to keep him going in the morass. He won, but only just, and the doubters in the English racing fraternity began to turn their attention once more to Petingo, and Noel Murless's main candidate, the huge Connaught.

As far as Lester was concerned, they could fancy who they liked. He had no doubts. He was sure Sir Ivor was at least three to four pounds better than Petingo and while he didn't yet know what his range would be, he knew that, over a mile, he was sitting on a Ferrari.

At Warren Place, Noel Murless completed final preparations with the exasperating Connaught. The colt's aversion to starting stalls was well known, but Murless hoped he had overcome that through a combination of cunning and persistence. He wasn't, however, convinced that Connaught was quite 2,000 Guineas material at this stage of the season. Sam Armstrong, on the other hand, couldn't have been happier. Petingo was eating well and working brilliantly. The racing press, while noting some capacity for improvement in Sir Ivor, had considered Petingo's Craven Stakes prep race the more impressive performance. The general public ignored them all. Piggott was on Sir Ivor, so that's where their money would go. On the course the book went 11/8 Sir Ivor, 9/4 Petingo – barely a pin between them.

Newmarket Heath can be a cheerless place, even in early spring, with North Sea winds to slap the face and sting the eyes. But, for once, a pale sun had decided to grace the scene and the air crackled with anticipation.

On the morning of the big race, Michael Phillips told readers of *The Times*, 'This is the most absorbing clash of personalities since Tudor Minstrel and Petition tried conclusions on this course in 1947.' (On that occasion, Tudor Minstrel had gone to post 11/8 favourite while Petition, at 5/2, was warmly fancied by his connections. As they came into line, Petition had made a sudden bolt, crashed into the tapes and unshipped his rider. He was remounted but made no showing in the race and was later found to have injured himself quite badly. He was off the racecourse until July while Tudor Minstrel, with Gordon Richards aboard, won in a canter by eight lengths.)

Petition was Petingo's sire. Now the son could make dramatic amends.

Concluding his piece, Phillips wrote: 'Petingo has always struck me, more so than Sir Ivor, as being the typical classic miler. With tenuous form links with which to compare the two, my forecast is a matter of opinion. Rightly or wrongly, I think Petingo will win. It now remains to be seen whether or not Piggott has the last laugh . . . '

Lester's pre-race summary was more succinct. 'Sir Ivor will eat him for breakfast!'

They were off at 3.38. So Blessed shot from the stalls as if he'd been stung, with the giant Connaught barely a stride behind. Two furlongs out, Petingo's jockey, Joe Mercer, found himself caught up in this helter-skelter of a gallop as his mount fought for his head. Piggott, by contrast, would have none of it. He tucked Sir Ivor in on the rails and waited.

By the six furlong pole, Connaught had gone and So Blessed began coming down through the gears. Inside the final furlong, Petingo took it up in the centre of the course. He looked, for a moment, to have made the decisive break. But Vincent O'Brien, watching from in front of the stands, thought otherwise. He could see Sir Ivor, still tightly held, improving on the rails, and a second later Piggott let him go.

The colt quickened dramatically. Piggott, his whip held high in his right hand, came upsides of Petingo with 150 yards to go, and two short taps were all he needed for the colt to lengthen his stride still further as the roar from the grandstand engulfed the runners. Sir Ivor passed the post a length and a half clear, and going away. Petingo stayed on gamely to finish second ahead of the fast-finishing Jimmy Reppin, a horse that later confirmed the form by becoming an outstanding miler in his own right.

O'Brien had landed his first 2,000 Guineas, Piggott his second, and both maestro and wizard exchanged smiles as wide as the Irish Sea as they were reunited in the unsaddling enclosure.

'Were you pleased?' asked O'Brien.

'Yes,' replied Piggott.

'*Very* pleased?' persisted the trainer.

'*Very* pleased!' confirmed his jockey, with an impish grin.

The worried trainer had heard all he needed to hear. They would go to the Derby and they would go as firm favourites, despite niggling doubts about Sir Ivor's stamina over the longer trip. The colt was immediately backed down to 4/5 for the Epsom classic.

Sir Ivor's owner, Raymond Guest, had always relied heavily on his trainer's judgement, that same trainer who had landed Larkspur as a 22/1 shot in the infamous Derby of 1962 when seven horses, including the favourite, fell coming out of Tattenham Corner. Larkspur was no Sir Ivor, so if O'Brien said this colt could win, that was more than enough for Guest. Shortly before the Grand Criterium in 1967, the owner had struck an each-way bet with bookmaker William Hill for £500 at 100/1 for the 1968 Derby. It was beginning to look like a shrewd investment.

The race had taken little out of Sir Ivor. He returned in triumph to Ireland and his subsequent work on the gallops at Ballydoyle pleased his trainer enormously. There would be no more outings before that Epsom date on 29 May, but there would be plenty of quiet, careful preparation for the colt that was already being whispered about as 'The horse of the century'.

By a happy coincidence, 1968 was the year a small, independent film company had chosen to begin production on a sports documentary film to be called *The Classics*. The script was to be written by award-winning sports writer Hugh McIlvaney of *The Observer*, with Richard Baerlein retained as racing consultant.

'It was the first real film on racing,' recalls Baerlein. 'No

one had ever tried to focus in so closely before, or go behind
the scenes in the preparation of a racehorse for a major race.
It was supposed to be just about the classics but, of course, it
turned out to be something very different indeed.'

What it became was *The Year of Sir Ivor*, a pulsating, highly
literate documentary that was to scoop top prizes
everywhere it was shown, including the top award at the
Grenoble Sports Film Festival. It has never been bettered,
but the producers would be the first to admit that they were
fortunate in their choice of collaborator.

'Technically, the crew were superb film-makers,' said
Baerlein, 'but they didn't know a lot about horse-racing.
After Sir Ivor won the Guineas and looked like winning the
Derby, they got prepared for making the film "The Year of
Sir Ivor" and so we went to Ballydoyle to film O'Brien and
the horse in training. The crew were setting up on the gallops
and working out angles and worrying about the light and so
on and someone said, "Well, if we don't get the picture right
this time we'll try it from over there," and so on.

' "Look," I said, "Sir Ivor is going to go down and come up
— once. It is being trained for the Derby and if you don't get
it, you've had it." They got it!'

Meanwhile, back at Newmarket and far removed from the
tranquillity of Tipperary, that other master trainer, Noel
Murless, was wrestling with a problem that had driven him
almost to the point of despair. His Derby hope, Connaught,
was proving a real handful.

He knew Connaught had some good races in him, but
what could you do with an animal that one day refused to
enter the starting stalls and the next left them so quickly that
he was a totally spent force by the time the others really
started racing? In his biography of Murless, Fitzgeorge
Parker provides an amusing postscript to Connaught's
Guineas flop.

Murless explains how he finally cured Connaught's starting stall jitters after the colt had yet again failed to co-operate
before the start of the classic trial Greenham Stakes at Newbury:

I took him home and got permission to use the stalls on the racecourse at Newmarket. I would put him in the stalls, jump him off, let him gallop for about a furlong and a half, pull up, go back and do it again. We would do that quite a few times and he became good at it. So good that in the 2,000 Guineas he went straight into the stalls, jumped off, galloped about a furlong and a half and tried to pull up! I was so furious with him that I said I'd send him down to the vet's, have him castrated and send him jumping . . .

He didn't, of course. Instead, that infinitely patient man sent him to Chester five days later where he gave such a good account of himself in the one-and-a-half miles Chester Vase that Murless concluded his colt really was a live Derby candidate.

The public seemed to think so too, as did the bookmakers. He would go to the post at 100/9, third favourite behind Sir Ivor and Remand.

And what of Petingo, Sam Armstrong's hope for a first 2,000 Guineas? He failed again in his next outing, the Prix Lupin in Paris, but then went on to win the St James's Palace Stakes over a mile at Ascot. He won the Sussex Stakes, too, at Goodwood, but was well beaten by the 2,000 Guineas third, Jimmy Reppin (receiving 6 lb), in the Wills Mile, also at Goodwood. After that, the so-called Wonder Horse was retired to stud where he sired two good winners – Fair Salina, 1978 Oaks, and English Prince, 1974 Irish Sweeps Derby – but he died young.

On the world scene in that early summer of 1968, the headlines were suddenly monopolized by the French. It was the year of the students' revolt in Paris with the German-born Daniel Cohn-Bendt ('Danny the Red') taking refuge in the barricaded Sorbonne while President de Gaulle threatened to ring the city with tanks and troops.

Back at home, Beatle John Lennon was being busted on a charge of possessing marijuana (along with a Mrs Yoko Ono Cox, as the papers coyly described her). The Labour Party seemed in disarray as Harold Wilson and James Callaghan clashed over policy and bookmakers were up in arms over the government's decision to levy them on turnover in future instead of profits. Betting tax also went up to 5 per cent.

Still, there was the European Cup Final between Manchester United and Benfica to look forward to, the first time an English club had been able to get so far. It was to be played on Derby Day, 29 May, and punters were being invited by William Hill's to link Manchester United with Derby hopeful Remand at 15/2. Some hope, though Manchester United at least obliged.

Epsom was its usual swirl of noise and colour when the big day arrived. Summer had broken out with a vengeance and the heat in the grandstand, packed to the rafters with Irishmen, was unbearable. They had come to see their favourite, Sir Ivor, carry off the biggest prize in racing, and they came not in hope but glorious expectation.

Lester Piggott continued to have doubts about his colt's ability to get the one-and-a-half-mile trip around the tortuous Epsom circuit, but to look at him you would never have known it. Old Stoneface was at his least fathomable, barely a flicker of light in those pale blue eyes as he marched briskly from the jockeys' weighing room into the paddock.

By contrast, Vincent O'Brien seemed like a man who'd picnicked too long on an ant hill. His nervousness was palpable but it didn't communicate itself to the magnificent racehorse whose coat positively glowed in the warm sunshire. Sir Ivor would have carried off the top prize in any equine *concours d'élégance* that day – but the same was not true of his rival, Remand.

Dick Hern's hope looked suspiciously light and was clearly fretful. Lines of worry were etched on jockey Joe Mercer's sanguine face. Remand's stable had been stricken with a coughing virus early in the season and Hern had positively nursed his charge towards Epsom, keeping him well isolated from potential sufferers and guarding his box as if it contained the crown jewels. Which in a way it did, if Remand could be first past the post.

In *The Times*, Michael Phillips had one final fling at betting against Sir Ivor, this time quoting an unlikely source to back his judgement. 'I believe,' he wrote, 'that Remand not only can win but will win, and it is encouraging to know that my barber, that fine judge, thinks likewise.' His idea of the finish was: 1, Remand; 2, Connaught; 3, Sir Ivor.

This time, Lester Piggott said nothing.

The preliminaries, always a welcome part of the Derby scene, seemed interminable that day, but finally they were off, with the blinkered Benroy taking them up the hill to the mile post before giving way to Murless's Connaught. The Newmarket maestro had clearly decided that Connaught's best chance lay in making it a true gallop and running the finishing speed out of Sir Ivor. But Piggott was too canny a campaigner for that. He resolutely tucked Sir Ivor into the pack and as they came round Tattenham Corner he was lying eighth.

So far, everything had gone according to plan, but as they came into the home straight Connaught quickened perceptibly, leaving Society, Atopolis, Laureate and the unfortunate Remand struggling to remain on terms. And Sir Ivor? He was behind the lot of them. The crowd became uneasy. Even Bull Hancock, whose shrewd eye had first discerned classic potential in the overgrown juvenile, turned away in despair.

As they entered the final furlong, Sandy Barclay had Connaught moving in a beautifully rhythmic run which seemed certain to carry them to victory. But as the winning post beckoned, Piggott, icy calm in the crisis, moved Sir Ivor out, balanced him and then asked for some overdrive. The response was so electrifying that those who saw it then, and have subsequently seen it re-run a hundred times on the film, still cannot believe it. As Lester was to say, 'In a few strides it was all over.'

Poor Sandy Barclay. The young, nineteen-year-old Scot who had inherited the mantle of Lester Piggott at the most powerful racing stable in England had ridden the perfect race and seen the chalice of victory dashed from his lips. He was puzzled, he was confused, and finally, he was tearful. He sat weeping in the weighing room. 'It was as though they had just jumped in,' he told the press. 'I really thought that I must win when we were just a furlong from home. I couldn't believe it when Lester and Sir Ivor came up alongside us.'

Raymond Guest couldn't believe it either, though he was five hundred miles away in County Wexford in Ireland. Official business, the planting of a commemorative tree at the Kennedy Memorial, had forced him to miss the most important day in his calendar. The event was a formal one, though far less solemn than he'd feared as the assembled dignitaries willingly agreed to a postponement of the actual ceremony while they gathered round a crackling portable radio relaying the race live from England. 'And Sir Ivor wins it!' came the disembodied voice from England while the cheers rang out all over southern Ireland.

Not many owners are given to win a Derby; fewer still claim that elusive prize twice. And Guest's astonishing luck would not end with Sir Ivor, for later he would claim the two biggest prizes in National Hunt racing, the Cheltenham Gold Cup and the Grand National, with that gutsy jumper L'Escargot. And don't forget that cheque for £62,500, courtesy of William Hill. Guest was truly a winner on the grand scale.

Lester had now landed his twelfth classic in fourteen years and he hadn't done with 1968 yet. There was still the St Leger ahead and a very real chance of pulling off the top European prize, the Prix de l'Arc de Triomphe, if Sir Ivor could get the tough, one-and-three-quarter-mile trip. Not that anyone doubted the severity of that task. Awaiting him in Paris would be Vaguely Noble, a brilliant animal – perhaps one of the greatest racehorses of all time – but something of a breeding freak in the eyes of most students of pedigree. Which underlines the point appreciated so shrewdly by Bull Hancock in Kentucky all those races ago. Somewhere along the line, you just have to back judgement against breeding, and his judgement had proved inspired.

Now it was the turn of Liam Ward to partner the wonder colt on his beloved Curragh in the Irish Sweeps Derby, a race O'Brien has always maintained is a classic in every sense of the word and not, as some would have it, a Celtic substitute for 'the real thing'. Naturally enough, the Irish were out in force to hail their champion and there was no reason to suppose that an upset might be on the cards.

Lester Piggott had been retained to ride Ribero for the American millionaire Charles Engelhard and he travelled to Ireland more in hope than expectation. Like all sons of the incomparable Ribot, Ribero was unpredictable, and he certainly wasn't in the class of his brother Ribocco who had given Piggott such thrilling success the summer before. But trainer Fulke Johnson Houghton believed in him despite a twelve-lengths drubbing by Connaught at Ascot, and Lester was happy to acknowledge that Ribero's one prime asset was sheer courage.

But at the Curragh the matter of sheer speed was likely to determine the outcome, and this was the quality Sir Ivor possessed in spades. Naturally, the bookmakers made their Epsom hero 1/3 on, while Ribero could manage no better than 100/6. Lester decided his tactics should be those of Noel Murless and Connaught at Epsom – go a fast gallop and try and leak the finish out of Sir Ivor. The question mark over the Irish colt's stamina was still there.

There was a slight delay at the start and when the horses did finally get off they went at just the pace Lester had hoped. Unlike Epsom, the Curragh is a flat, galloping course and wide open. You can't tuck an animal in so readily, especially if the field is truly racing, and as they entered the straight Ribero was into a powerful stride just a touch behind the leaders, Stitch and Giolla Mear.

As they came inside the final two furlongs, Ward, who had improved from last to second, seemed about to launch his challenge, but Piggott, sensing the moment Ward would press the accelerator, drove Ribero still harder. The move gave them first run and Ward suddenly had work to do.

A furlong from home and both Piggott and Ward were working like dervishes on their animals, but Lester's instinctive break was now looking decisive. In the vast crowd, the cheering stopped. There was a stunned silence as thousands of betting slips suddenly became so much used paper. Ribero, still running on as if its lungs would burst with the effort, flashed past the post two lengths to the good. Ward drooped visibly in the saddle. O'Brien looked like a mourner at a wake.

Whatever elation Lester felt at yet another amazing piece of smash-and-grab riding, he kept to himself. His expression mirrored the puzzlement felt all around the Curragh. 'Two furlongs out I looked over my shoulder and saw Sir Ivor was cantering. I thought I was looking at the winner but all of a sudden he started going back. I was surprised my horse went so well and won so easily.'

Ward said simply, 'He just died in my hands. He went to pieces on me a furlong and a half out.' A close study of the film of the race shows just how decisive that early move of Lester's had been. Ribero's response to his jockey's sudden urging was the last thing a tiring racehorse could have wanted. Sir Ivor seemed to sense there was just too much to do and no amount of flailing from Ward or any other rider was going to conjure up a winning response.

Once again, Ribero's ebullient owner, Charles Engelhard, had missed the *coup de grâce*. Just as when Ribero had upset the odds in 1967, the American was on a river fishing trip in Canada. 'He will be bewildered,' said Engelhard's racing manager David McCall, who had predicted no better than third place for his owner's charge.

At first, it was suggested that Sir Ivor might be suffering from a bug picked up in England and O'Brien agreed there was such a possibility. But when his team returned to Ballydoyle and Sir Ivor ate up as heartily as ever, it was clear that a deeper factor must be at work: that suspect strain in his breeding which had always suggested this was a racehorse that only got a mile and a half in certain conditions – and those conditions did not include a true gallop. He might also be tired, suggested Ward, and O'Brien, who was himself tired after the emotional strain of the day, was forced to agree.

Lester returned to England happy in the knowledge that he not only had another major notch on his totem of major prizes but also that Johnson Houghton had provided him with another genuine candidate for the Doncaster St Leger in October. Meanwhile, he was surprised and delighted to receive a call from O'Brien saying that Sir Ivor had recovered well enough from his exertions to be a certain runner in

Sandown's Eclipse Stakes the following week and Piggott would be his jockey. This mile-and-a-quarter trip, Lester had always asserted, was the colt's true distance and he viewed the prospect of yet another big prize with some relish.

But now, unexpectedly, it was Piggott who was to taste the bitter ashes of defeat. The going was exceptionally firm and the field contained two brilliant four-year-olds, 1967 Derby hero Royal Palace and the French flier Taj Dewan. As the horses turned into the finishing straight, Sir Ivor began to lose his action on the rock-solid surface. He was unable to stride out freely and Royal Palace and Taj Dewan quickly left the Irish contender adrift as they fought out a thrilling battle. Somehow, Sandy Barclay kept Royal Palace going to the line though every muscle seemed to scream in protest and, after a photo, Noel Murless's brilliant colt was given the verdict on the nod.

So what next for Sir Ivor? O'Brien thought long and hard. The ground at Sandown had 'jarred' Sir Ivor's knees but still he confounded the stable by working as well as ever when O'Brien eased him back on to the gallops. The three hard races in three weeks may have extended his resources temporarily, but they could never quench his competitive fire and it was clear the Arc de Triomphe was still very much within his scope.

Sir Ivor thrived on racing so O'Brien had no qualms about sending him to France for a prep race a week before the Longchamp classic. He chose the Prix Henri Delamare and once again Sir Ivor let him down, though he was hardly disgraced by finishing in second place. The stable reported that he came back 'blowing like a pig', so the outing had clearly been necessary though the blot on his racing record was suddenly growing longer. O'Brien, never one to panic, decided to work him gently in the quiet forests and wait patiently for the big day.

But if the golden touch had temporarily deserted Sir Ivor, it had descended on Lester Piggott in dramatic style. The Doncaster St Leger would see him reunited with Ribero though the two had crossed paths somewhat dramatically in the King George VI and Queen Elizabeth Stakes at Ascot in

July. On the way to the start, Ribero had suddenly become frisky and promptly unseated his perplexed rider before trotting away to nibble some grass and bushes by the Old Mile start. After that, he showed little interest in the race and Lester was forced to concede defeat long before the finish.

And just to prove that that cantankerous Ribot streak was still running strongly in his veins, Ribero failed to justify himself in his next race, the Prix Kergorlay at Deauville, in which Pardallo took the honours. Doncaster would be different, or so Lester and patient trainer Fulke Johnson Houghton hoped. And then, on the evening of the big race, the heavens opened and the Yorkshire course became a bog.

12 | *Ribero*

Doncaster is not the prettiest town in England. It is a muscular, no-nonsense sort of place with little to calm the spirit or soothe the eye. It needs sunshine to soften its raw, industrial edges. But on St Leger day all it could offer was cold, unremitting rain.

Even the charming Town Moor course, which lies in a kind of puzzled splendour to the east of the town, was shrouded in a moving curtain of water. The ground looked ominously soft and Lester knew he had a tough race ahead. But just how tough he couldn't guess until he'd had a chance to assess Ribero's fitness to run.

In the week leading up to the race, Ribero had developed that most painful of conditions in a racehorse, a mouth ulcer, which had seriously hampered trainer Fulke Johnson Houghton's final preparations. He was in any case an unpredictable character – a testimony to that good old cantankerous Ribot blood – but now he was so skittish that even his lad had trouble soothing him. Miraculously, in the early hours of race morning itself, the ulcer burst and peace and light suddenly flooded the land. Ribero was sore but ready to run. The rest would be up to Lester.

Surprisingly after his performance at the Curragh, Ribero was easy to back, drifting in the market from 5/2 to 100/30 at the off. Perhaps the punters were remembering the twelve-lengths beating the favourite, Connaught, had given Ribero in Ascot's King Edward VII Stakes. Lester knew all about

Connaught. He knew in particular that the giant colt liked the ground firm and fast. And he knew, too, that his old boss, Noel Murless, would be fretting and worrying as he prodded the yielding turf with his size twelve boots. It gave Lester a nice psychological edge.

There was a slight scare at the start as both Connaught and Ribero jibed at going into the stalls. In Ribero's case, there was an excuse. His mouth was desperately sore and handlers aren't always the most delicate of removal men. As for Connaught, he was just back to his old tricks and it took some rare skill on young Sandy Barclay's part to get him installed. When the gates finally opened, Ribero having once been coaxed in now had to be coaxed out and Lester lost a good ten lengths on the field in the first fifty yards.

It didn't matter. Scipio took them along at such a slow gallop in the early stages that Lester was soon able to put Ribero back in touch and settle him for the run-in. The pace remained a crawl right up until the final three furlongs when the give in the ground began to tell and Cold Storage, Alignment, Riboccare and Mount Athos quickly lost position. Mount Athos was in fact pulled up a moment later when his jockey, Ron Hutchinson, began to sense the animal might have suffered an injury. That left only Ribero, Canterbury and Connaught in contention and it was clear that Connaught was hating every second of it.

Inside the final furlong Lester made his move, stealing first run on Canterbury and Bill Williamson and establishing a three-length advantage before Canterbury was able to start reeling him in. Ribero was by now flagging badly, but he was giving everything it was possible to give, so instead of using his whip, Lester sat perfectly still. Stride by stride, Williamson closed the gap and at the line the verdict depended solely on which animal had got the nod.

Lester had no doubts. He steered Ribero firmly towards the winner's enclosure, and a few minutes later, confirmation came. The official distance was the lowest it's possible to give in racing, a short head. But an examination of the official photograph shows it was literally a matter of a nostril! On one thing everyone was agreed, Lester had ridden one of his most brilliant races ever.

Lester smiled that day. It was by now considered a rare enough event for it to be recorded in newspaper reports of his big race winners. It prompted Ribero's trainer to say later, 'We know that Lester is always reluctant to show his true feelings, but I sensed that day at Doncaster that he was very pleased with himself. I knew what he had done – and he knew what had been done. It was simply a brilliant piece of riding. There had been so much touch, so much feel. I can't imagine that anyone has ever ridden a better race. Really, the fellow defies the imagination.'

As it happened, Piggott's finest hour was also to mark Ribero's swansong as a celebrity. The partnership between the plucky colt and its ice-cool partner was now dissolved as Sir Ivor came galloping back into Lester's life. It was time to prepare for the Arc de Triomphe and the richest prize in Europe.

The press billed it as 'The Two Horse Race' and that wasn't far from the truth. Vaguely Noble, the French colt that was owned by a syndicate headed by Hollywood beauty surgeon Dr Robert Franklyn, had been preparing for months with just the Arc in mind. In Etienne Pollet he had a genius of a trainer whose Chantilly stables brimmed over with talent and had included the legendary Derby and Arc winner of 1965, Sea Bird II. Pollet knew precisely what it took to win this truest of middle-distance races and Vaguely Noble was trained to the minute.

Mind you, O'Brien had also saddled an Arc winner, the unlikely Ballymoss, in 1958, and he was in no doubt that Sir Ivor's conditioning was perfect. Stamina was another matter. The state of the going and the pace of the gallop would decide whether Sir Ivor could preserve enough of that famous pounce to beat his rival. Again, it was up to Lester. There were no riding orders from O'Brien.

The 'two horse race' proved to be just that despite a high-class field that included the blisteringly fast filly La Lagune, runaway winner of the English Oaks. It was clear by the first half-mile that Vaguely Noble had the measure of all its rivals – the only serious question was, did Sir Ivor have the measure of Vaguely Noble?

Lester decided to play a cat-and-mouse game, tracking

every move his rival made. As Michael Phillips later noted in *The Times*, 'Where Vaguely Noble went, Sir Ivor went: when Vaguely Noble went, Sir Ivor went. Vaguely Noble was always within striking distance. In fact [Piggott] never lay further back than sixth. In the role of private detective, Sir Ivor just tailed him.'

The moment of truth came in the short finishing straight. Bill Williamson pushed Vaguely Noble to the front, using nothing more than hands and heels, and he was still using hands and heels as they pounded into the final furlong. 'I must admit,' said Lester afterwards as he wryly studied a closed-circuit television recording of the finish, 'I would have given him a smack then!' Instead it was Sir Ivor that got the smack and although the colt responded with characteristic courage, it was always a forlorn gesture. 'Vaguely Noble really had twice as much in hand,' said the beaten jockey.

The verdict was three easy lengths and the Parisian crowd cheered to the echo as their champion flashed past the post. O'Brien, watching from the stand, was not really surprised by the ease of Vaguely Noble's victory. He knew a great racehorse when he saw one. But he was astonished at the way Sir Ivor stayed on. Four-year-old Carmarthen, who had battled gamely into third place with a punitive 9 st. 6 lb on his back, was a full four lengths adrift of the Irish colt. So what was all that about Sir Ivor's suspect stamina?

O'Brien wasn't the only onlooker to register the fact and in some cases those observations led them directly back to the jockey. Had Lester boobed? Did he try too hard to conserve Sir Ivor's finishing speed? It was a criticism Lester Piggott would hear again and again and one he would always counter with withering scorn. 'I get annoyed when people delve too much into theory, when they try to tell you what you should have done. There is only one place to be making decisions – that's out on the back of the horse. I know mistakes happen; sometimes you can get it wrong. But if you have enough experience, if you have thought about the race, I really think you are the best judge of what needs doing.'

Sir Ivor returned to Ireland, not in disgrace but not quite a hero either. Those plaudits for the wonder horse were beginning to sound more hollow and it was a point that niggled O'Brien and owner Raymond Guest. So why not give Sir Ivor a chance to redeem his reputation? Two possible races appealed. The first was the Champion Stakes at Newmarket to be run over one and a quarter miles – still, in Lester's view, Sir Ivor's optimum distance. The second was the prestigious Washington International in which the cream of Europe and the cream of America had a rare chance to come together on turf over the classic middle distance of one and a half miles.

At Newmarket Sir Ivor's main challenge would again come from France, this time in the shape of Taj Dewan who had fought that epic photo-finish battle with 1967 Derby winner Royal Palace in the Eclipse Stakes at Newmarket in July. The three-quarters of a length between favourite Sir Ivor and Taj Dewan that day had seemed a false reflection to O'Brien of their respective merits and he itched for a chance of revenge. Even so, the French horse was ominously fresh, having been rested since in readiness for this final battle.

It was in every sense a dramatic day. British racegoers flocked to the home of racing to bid a fond farewell to their adopted hero. Raymond Guest had already decided to retire Sir Ivor at three and send him to stud in Ireland for a year before returning him to stand in America. It might also be his last race ever because, despite the temptation, no firm decision had been reached on the Washington engagement. Lester was as ready to race as anyone.

Yves St Martin on Taj Dewan opted to let his colt do much of the running. They were questionable tactics and by the time the field reached the Bushes, the French horse was visibly tiring. This time Lester didn't wait. He shot Sir Ivor to the front with such little effort that it was all over well before the final furlong. Locris and Candy Cane trailed in a remote second and third, while all over Newmarket the cheers rang out for Lester and Sir Ivor. Of all the many triumphs, this had been the most emphatic.

Three hard races in three weeks would have taken the bloom off most racehorses, but Sir Ivor seemed so little affected by his exertions that Guest and O'Brien quickly agreed that Washington was a live proposition. They decided to rest the colt for a week and review the situation, but there never much doubt in either mind that he would be ready.

And so, the Sir Ivor story came to a truly sensational climax by the freezing waters of the Potomac, three thousand miles from the rolling meadows of his adopted Ireland.

In his *Observer* article of the morning of 10 November, Richard Baerlein painted a vivid picture of just what was in store for both horse and rider. 'Lester Piggott's responsibilities to the public in England and America for the race on Monday,' he wrote, 'are incalculable. His appearance at Laurel could make the difference between victory and defeat for Sir Ivor.'

Baerlein went on to reveal how O'Brien's meticulous preparations had led him to import Irish drinking water for the colt, but 'that has now dried up and they have had to send for some spring water at Arkansas to take its place. The Maryland water is not considered good enough for horses,' he added. 'Or humans.' And on the likely going he wrote, 'No one agrees on the going here at the moment. Some call it soft, some heavy. I think it would be called fast going in England, with no semblance of jar. If the same ground existed in France they would start up the sprinklers right away.'

It was against such vivid word pictures, which would have the British and Irish public glued to their radio sets, that the great man himself jetted into Washington and his last working meeting with the animal that he was happy to describe as 'the greatest'.

The American press were not too familiar with 'this Piggott'. And they certainly weren't familiar with his style of riding. In the States, most races were hustle and bustle dirt-track affairs with devil take the hindmost and the ticking clock the only true criterion of performance. They were to learn, of course. And they didn't like it one bit.

In the event the going was much softer than Baerlein had predicted and it was to have a significant influence on Lester's reading of the race. The Japanese horse, Takeshiba-O, accepted early pacemaking duties with the American second favourite, Czar Alexander, in hot pursuit. Sir Ivor was away in sixth and Lester kept him there as the early stages of the battle unfolded and the French colt Petrone and the other fancied American challenger, Fort Marcy, moved into the picture.

Down the back stretch and Carmarthen moved into a challenging position on the wide outside. Lester appeared to be searching for a gap on the rails but none appeared, and to the nail-biting dismay of the British press corps, Sir Ivor was suddenly relegated to last.

Three furlongs to go.

Around the home turn and now it was the Americans fighting it out with Carmarthen still poised and Lester still searching for daylight. For a second he thought he'd found it as Czar Alexander and Fort Marcy momentarily drifted apart but it was simply a mirage, and suddenly they were inside the final furlong.

Two hundred yards – and Lester pounced.

In half a dozen breathtaking strides he shot Sir Ivor to the outside and then pressed the accelerator as he had never pressed it before. The colt simply exploded to the front leaving the American challengers leaden-footed in his wake. He passed the post with a mere three-quarters of a length to spare – six feet of nothing – but it brought home the bacon and sent the British contingent into paroxysms of delight. As Vincent O'Brien exulted later, 'Once he got the opening it was "ping". '

The Americans didn't see it that way at all. As they crowded into the press interview room after the race, the atmosphere was charged with hostility. 'Why had he left it so late?' they demanded. 'Hadn't he ridden a really bum race?' At first, Piggott was nonplussed. Then he became angry and finally stormed from the meeting to the sanctuary of the changing room where wiser counsel prevailed. To the British press he gave a balanced picture.

'I had a little trouble getting through,' he admitted. 'The patchy softness in places meant he kept drifting away from me. I thought he'd do it easier than he did. I think I would have won by 100 yards if the ground had not been soft.'

It was good enough for the British but not for the Americans, now with a Piggott snub to add fuel to their anger. Next day, the reports were vitriolic.

'It was the worst ride I've ever seen,' a top American jockey told the *Washington Post*. 'He was running up horses' rear ends all the way round. He should a' won by 15 lengths.' Another: 'If he were an American jockey he'd be crucified.' And still another: 'He flayed Sir Ivor from the eight furlong post to the winning post.'

Not exactly pretty stuff, and there is no doubt that even Lester was stung. He played it down then and he plays it down today. 'They said some stupid things, but then I suppose they have a job to do and I'm not too worried about how they do it. When you have been doing the same thing for twenty years you ride along with the praise and the criticism. I have won by a short head after making a hell of a mess of things and then read of my brilliance. At other times, I have done everything right, just got done on the post and read that I made a hash of everything. They slammed me after I won with Sir Ivor, but I just couldn't accept their criticism because I didn't think they were qualified to make judgements. I knew a bit more about Sir Ivor than they did. I knew what I had to do.'

It seems the right postscript to a chapter in Lester's life that scaled the heights and, just occasionally, skirted the depths as well. Sir Ivor provided some of the golden moments that he will take into retirement and they will dazzle the disappointments into insignificance. The same is probably true of another great horse that Piggott rode to ecstasy and despair. But in November 1968 they hadn't even met. That was still very much in the future . . .

13 | *Nijinsky*

Charles Engelhard was a big roly-poly of a man with a fruity upper-class New York accent. He was part of the American aristocracy, in so far as America can be said to have such a thing; a graduate of St Paul's and Princeton, scion of Manhattan's exclusive Brook Club. He was also ferociously wealthy.

The Engelhard Minerals and Chemical Corporation traded in diamonds, silver, platinum, and – above all – gold. At one time, Engelhard practically cornered the world market in gold, an achievement which inspired James Bond author Ian Fleming to create his famous character, Goldfinger. Engelhard was the prototype in theory only. Unlike Fleming's character, Charles Engelhard was a jolly, almost avuncular figure. And he was popular in racing circles where he had built an empire to rival his minerals operation.

England was its centre, with horses in training at four separate establishments, while others were trained in France, Ireland, the USA and South Africa. But it wasn't just his purchasing power that had made Engelhard successful enough to win classic races on both sides of the Irish Sea. He was a good judge of horses and an even better judge of men. Lester Piggott had twice reaped the benefit of Engelhard's pursuit of the Ribot bloodline with victories in the English and Irish St Legers on Ribocco and Ribero, and it was the obsession with Ribot colts that was to lead

Engelhard to the greatest racehorse of this century.

Vincent O'Brien's American connections had become well established through his friendship with James Cox Brady, chairman of the New York Racing Association. A Brady introduction was, according to O'Brien, the 'seal of approval' on the other side of the Atlantic, so it was no surprise when Engelhard approached the Tipperary wizard in 1966 and asked him to cast his eye over a Ribot colt that was coming up at the Woodbine yearling sales in Canada. O'Brien agreed to make the 7,000-mile trip from Ballydoyle, although, as he said later, 'It seemed an awful long way to go just to see one horse.'

It seemed an awful lot further after one look at the Ribot colt. It had a crooked foreleg. His trip had been wasted. Still, the luck of the Irish can prevail in even the most trying circumstances and the trainer decided to stay on and watch the rest of the show – 'just in case'.

O'Brien found his crock of gold all right.

'He really filled my eye,' is his charming description of that first sight of Nijinsky. 'He struck me as having the *makings* of a good horse.'

On examining his pedigree, O'Brien found that the colt came from the second crop of Northern Dancer, a top-class American which had come within an ace of capturing the fabled Triple Crown. Northern Dancer had won the Kentucky Derby and Preakness Stakes but just failed to stay the more testing Belmont Stakes, finishing third. The dam was Flaming Page – big, rangy, temperamental, but a proven winner over a mile and a quarter. It looked a useful mating, one that suggested speed rather than stamina. But you never know . . .

Next, O'Brien flew down to Saratoga to meet Charles Engelhard at that Royal Ascot of North American racing, the July Meeting. Engelhard was impressed by O'Brien's enthusiasm for the Northern Dancer colt and agreed to bid for him. The trainer left America a happy man. He would have been considerably less happy had he known what was going on behind the scenes.

Nijinsky's breeder, Canadian tycoon E. P. Taylor, was

proclaiming his colt's potential to anyone who would listen, and one who did was Garfield Weston, owner of Fortnum and Mason. Weston mounted a high-powered expedition to look over the horse. As well as a top vet, he invited Noel Murless's brother Stuart to accompany him.

When news of the 'raiding party' reached a nervous O'Brien back home in Tipperary, he was already worrying himself sick at Engelhard's plans to send an anonymous aide to bid for Nijinsky in the sale ring, to camouflage his interest. The man chosen had no experience in thse matters. It was so easy to make a slip . . . Now there was Weston to worry about.

In the event, he didn't have to worry long. Stuart Murless decided the big colt would take too long to come to hand and Weston was persuaded to invest elsewhere. Still, Taylor's confident trumpeting had had its effect, and when the Toronto sales opened the ring was packed with potential bidders for the Northern Dancer colt. Bidding was brisk, sweeping past the 60,000 dollar mark until sticking in the low eighties. Whatever happened, it would be a new Canadian record price. Finally, at 84,000 dollars, the colt was knocked down to a gentleman from Newark, New Jersey. Engelhard had got his horse!

Now the fun began.

That quality, that potential for greatness, that O'Brien had spotted in the colt was first to manifest itself in a wilful temperament. Nijinsky was just plain unco-operative, showing flashes of temper if a favoured routine was broken and frequently reluctant to leave the warmth of his box for a cold gallop in the winter half-light.

In their book *Vincent O'Brien's Great Horses*, Jacqueline O'Brien and Ivor Herbert reveal how crucial the sensitive handling of senior work riders Johnny Brabston and Danny O'Sullivan was to the horse's progession. 'Nijinsky could so easily have been spoiled,' Vincent O'Brien states. 'They had the strength to handle him and the patience not to knock him about.' Gradually, Nijinsky came to love the competitive spins on the lush Ballydoyle turf. He went as 'sweetly as a hunter' when in full gallop. And when it came time to school him in breaking fast from the starting stalls, he took to the challenge with enthusiasm.

The bush telegraph was soon tuned in and when O'Brien decided he was ready for his first trial on the racecourse in the Erne Stakes at the Curragh, the Irish bookmaking fraternity had him a solid 4/11. Their prudence was justified. Nijinsky was never off the bit as Liam Ward coaxed him into the lead just before the post. The verdict was half a length – not an earth-shattering margin, merely enough.

Next came the Railway Stakes (6 f. 63 yd), also at the Curragh, the Anglesey Stakes (6 f. 63 yd) and finally the top two-year-old trial, the one-mile Beresford Stakes. He won them all handily, although Decies asked him to do a little bit more over the longer distance and that horse later proved its class by winning the Irish 2,000 Guineas.

O'Brien was satisfied, and so was Lester Piggott, who'd slipped into Ballydoyle on a flying visit earlier in the summer to assess the potential wonder colt. After a brief gallop he returned to give his verdict: 'He'll do.' It was pure Piggott, and while the stable lads – who had by now taken Nijinsky firmly to their hearts – might have wished for a little more hyperbole, it was enough for O'Brien.

Liam Ward was O'Brien's first jockey in Ireland, but both trainer and owner had Piggott in mind for the big prize, the 1970 Derby. It had therefore been agreed that the two would share rides, with Piggott having the mount in England and France. It was a curious arrangement, but it worked.

Nijinsky crossed the Irish Sea for the first time in October to contest the seven-furlong Dewhurst Stakes at Newmarket. It was to be his last outing as a two-year-old and a firm pointer to his potential for the classic campaign the following season. Now, for the first time, the English racing public were to find out what all the fuss was about as Nijinsky cruised home by three lengths from Recalled and Sandal. The prize money of £10,576 made a sizeable dent in the $84,000 price tag.

Up until the Dewhurst, which established Nijinsky as ante-post favourite for both the 2,000 Guineas and the Derby, Piggott had been toying with the idea of partnering

Left: Lester at 15, hauling tack in his father's Lambourn yard with another hopeful young apprentice
(*Sport and General*)

Below: Striding out on his 1952 Derby mount Gay Time, so cruelly beaten on the line by Charlie Smirke's Tulyar
(*Sport and General*)

The wonder filly Petite Etoile led in by owner Prince Aly Khan after slaughtering her rivals in the 1959 Oaks (*Sport and General*)

Racing's wedding of the year in 1960, Susan Armstrong and Lester Piggott celebrate in traditional manner for the benefit of the press (*Sport and General*)

St Paddy, one of the most significant horses in the Piggott legend, carried
Lester to victory in the 1960 Derby and St Leger (shown here)
(*Sport and General*)

The Horse of the Century. Nijinsky completes the Triple Crown with victory in the 1970 St Leger at Doncaster (*Gerry Cranham*)

Above: Colourful Eygptian-born trainer Maurice Zilber shares in Lester's triumph after saddling little fancied Empery to win the 1976 Derby (*Gerry Cranham*)

Above right: One of Lester's most dramatic Derby wins came on The Minstrel when holding off Willie Carson and Hot Grove by a neck in the 1977 classic (*Gerry Cranham*)

Right: A unique shot from the rails side of Alleged and Lester Piggott striding to victory at Longchamp in the 1977 Prix de L'Arc de Triomphe (*Gerry Cranham*)

A combination that flared all too briefly, champion trainer Henry Cecil and Lester discuss tactics on the gallops at Newmarket (*Gerry Cranham*)

Lester Piggott has come a long way since the days when cigars were his only diet. Now they are a luxury he can indulge at his whim, for Britain's most successful jockey ever is also its wealthiest, a millionaire several times over (*Express Newspapers*)

the French horse Breton in the Epsom classic. Such thoughts were abandoned long before he'd passed the finishing post. Nijinsky may not have given him the same warm feeling as his beloved Sir Ivor, but it had given him as much power. Perhaps more. He knew he was on to another winner.

During the winter, no hiccups were reported in Nijinsky's preparation, although O'Brien's blacksmith, Davy Walsh, was later to recall a twisted hock that kept him off the gallops for two weeks. But when the colt reappeared on the Curragh in the spring for his prep race, the Gladness Stakes, he was as full of himself as ever and toyed with the field before landing the £2,000 first prize.

As 2,000 Guineas day approached, the English bookmakers began to look a little careworn. It was freely estimated that they would lose between them upwards of £500,000 if Nijinsky won, with Ladbrokes alone in for about £110,000. Their only possible response was to discourage any further betting and from 3/1 at the start of the season, Nijinsky was quoted at 4/7 by the day of the race.

In a memorable headline on 29 April 1970, the *Sporting Life* asked simply: 'WHO'S GOING TO BE SECOND TO NIJINSKY?' It seemed the only question worth asking.

The answer turned out to be Yellow God, who was coaxed into a challenging position by Australian Bill Williamson, only for Piggott to press the accelerator in the last half-furlong and cruise in by two and a half lengths. The bookmakers took their caning but didn't learn their lesson. Instead of shortening the odds still further, they allowed the wonder horse to go to post a generous 11/8 against, a price I, for one, duly snapped up. The 2,000 Guineas had been my first sight of Nijinsky and it was a sight I'd never seen on a racecourse before. It was simply electrifying.

Perhaps it was that blinding impression of speed that was to muddy perspective in the weeks leading up to the Epsom Derby and persuade normally sane men like William Hill to doubt Nijinsky's staying power. His pedigree was suddenly the subject of close scrutiny and what it revealed wasn't entirely complimentary. Northern Dancer emphatically had *not* stayed the one and a half miles of the Belmont Stakes and

Flaming Page had only been proven over a mile and a quarter.

Then there was the matter of Etienne Pollet's postponed retirement.

The master French trainer had in his yard a big, gangling colt named Gyr which was sensationally fast and, having been sired by the legendary Sea Bird, of proven stamina. Pollet was so sure he had a potential Derby winner on his hands that he postponed plans to retire just so that he could have a final tilt at the ultimate classic. Finally, he chose Bill Williamson to partner Gyr and no one doubted the Australian's ability to negotiate the roller-coaster downs of Epsom.

But could the horse? It really was a brute of an animal, long in the leg and with enormous reach. It was hard to visualize it tiptoeing around the infamous Tattenham Corner, which Willie Shoemaker vividly describes as 'a skating rink'. But there were plenty who could. Lester Piggott's closest friend among the jockeys, the late Brian Taylor, told Claude Duval in the *Sun* that 'Gyr is a brilliant colt. He always comes good for the big occasion. Gyr will trot up.'

The prediction brought a wry smile to the lips of his friend resting at home in Newmarket. Five days earlier, the question of whether Piggott could steer home Nijinsky had been rendered almost academic. Piggott had collapsed after the second race and it was clear to all who'd seen his pale, skeletal face that he had taken his battle with the scales a stage too far. After treatment in the medical room he emerged, still ashen-faced, to announce that he would be taking a break, he would not ride again before the Derby. The decision came as a blessed relief, not only to Nijinsky's connections but also to the racing press who saw him every day and had become increasingly alarmed at his condition. But you didn't tell Lester Piggott when to stop.

Meanwhile, Piggott's partner was enjoying the peace and tranquillity of Sandown Park, just a short drive from Epsom. O'Brien, the master of detailed planning, had decided that the greater security offered by the stabling facilities at Sandown would reduce the risk of nobbling and that the animal would appreciate being away from the hustle and bustle of

the Epsom carnival. But even the best-laid plans can be over-
turned on a sudden whim.

On the eve of the big race, Nijinsky and the team transferred to the racecourse stables at Epsom and the horse began
its final work-out. All seemed in order – a sharp, four-furlong
uphill sprint and then a gentle hack down the straight to the
winning post. But once back in his box, Nijinsky began to
sweat up. O'Brien began to sweat too – it looked as though
the horse had colic.

A local vet confirmed the diagnosis and the hours of anxious waiting began. O'Brien was facing another dilemma,
too. Should he inform the press? The memory of Larkspur
eight years earlier was still etched bitterly in his mind. On
that occasion, the animal had broken down in training a
week before the race and O'Brien, in fairness to the betting
public, announced that Larkspur was a doubtful starter.
That effectively ended any further ante-post interest. But
two days before the race, O'Brien's vet Bob Griffin pronounced Larkspur fit to run and he was reinstated in the
book. At this point, owner Raymond Guest began backing
the animal left, right and centre. And when Larkspur duly
trotted in after the infamous pile-up at Tattenham Corner in
which seven horses fell, the stewards deprived O'Brien of
that first sweet moment of triumph by summoning him to
explain the betting spree on a stated doubtful runner.

O'Brien was furious. The stewards promptly accepted his
explanation, of course, but that wasn't really the point. The
trainer felt he had been somehow victimized. And it was his
own honesty and concern for the punter that had placed him
in 'the dock'. He vowed then never to tell the press of his riding plans in advance.

Now, here he was just twenty-four hours from the Derby
facing the same crisis of conscience as he had eight years ago.
In the event, the decision was made for him. After a couple of
painful hours, pawing at his box and sweating, Nijinsky
seemed to relax slightly. Two of the lads collected some fresh
grass, mixed it with soda bicarbonate and a little bran, and
offered it to the horse. Nijinsky began to nibble. The crisis
was over. By the evening, he was full of himself again and

ready to do battle next day as the hot Derby favourite.

3 June was a day that will live for ever in the memory. The
crowd on the downs was estimated at close to a million and
the weather was sweltering, just as it had been two years
before for the triumph of that other wonder horse, Sir Ivor.
Charles Engelhard had flown in by private jet and, finding
that Nijinsky was only 11/8 in the market, he promptly
slapped £1,000 to win on his horse – 'to buy some drinks for
the lads'.

His confidence and that of millions of housewives who
were backing Lester first, Nijinsky second, seemed amply
justified in the parade ring. The Irish bay looked outstanding with only Approval, trained by a promising young newcomer called Henry Cecil, able to stand muster. And in the
lengthy preliminaries which are part of the Derby tradition,
Nijinsky and Piggott were as cool and imperturbable as if it
was a Sunday hack.

At the starting stalls, Nijinsky was equally well behaved,
but the highly fancied Gyr began to play up badly, and for a
long time refused to go in. Finally, he was installed and the
1970 Derby was under way.

Long Till and Cry Baby were the first to break, setting a
good gallop going up the hill with Lester and Nijinsky tucked
away towards the back of the eleven-horse field. It was a testimony to Nijinsky's clear dominance of his three-year-old
rivals that so few acceptors had been left in.

By Tattenham Corner, Nijinsky had improved to sixth
place but among those ahead of him was Gyr, who seemed to
be relishing the ups and downs. Williamson had the French
colt so beautifully balanced that, as Roger Mortimer later
wrote, 'he bowled down the hill like a polo pony'. Approval,
that other well-fancied contender, did not. Cecil's handsome
animal completely lost its action so that when the field
turned into the straight the only serious contenders left were
the leader, Great Wall, ridden by Joe Mercer, Long Till,
Gyr, Stintino and Nijinsky.

Two and a half furlongs from home, Gyr took it up and
with that ground-devouring stride looked all over a winner.
But Piggott had yet to make his move on Nijinsky. There

were more eyes on that famous bottom than on the leader's straining head as they passed the two furlong from home maker. Even Engelhard, whose normal response to the tension of seeing one of his horses run is to watch the expression on the face of his racing manager, simply had to look. His binoculars swept down the straight. Nijinsky was coming.

The murmur of anticipation became a rumble and finally a roar as Lester switched on the afterburner with two short taps of his whip. Nijinsky quickened instantly and within a few strides had cut his rival down. Inside the final furlong he seemed almost to be cantering, yet his time was to be the second fastest in the history of the race. It was a stunning, uplifting triumph, officially two and a half lengths but, in reality, the length of a street. There were no doubts about Nijinsky's stamina now.

For Lester Piggott, the man who had wasted himself to the point of collapse just a few days earlier, it was a supreme moment, one he was experiencing for the fifth time at Epsom – though never on a horse like this. Afterwards his summing up was simple: 'We were always cantering. A grand ride, a great horse.' O'Brien was more emphatic. 'He slammed them.'

And where was the man who had been willing to back the eye of his trainer and pay 84,000 dollars for an animal sight unseen? Sitting under one of the stairways in the grandstand drinking iced coke from a can. For Charles Engelhard it was the fulfilment of a dream nurtured in 1948 when he had watched his first Derby. 'I know now I was right to want it so badly,' said the perspiring owner as he struggled deeper into the comforting shade of the stairwell. 'Nijinsky is a wonderful animal. Lester Piggott is a wonderful jockey and Vincent O'Brien is a master of training. This is all too marvellous. I also met the Queen Mother!'

That meeting proved to be memorable for another reason. The stout Mr Engelhard had burst his braces during the excitement of the race and was presented to the royal party with his elbows pinned firmly into his sides. One false move and . . .

In the euphoria of the moment, Engelhard not unnaturally waxed lyrical on everything and, in particular, the partnership between man and horse. 'There is no way,' he said, 'I want to see Lester Piggott and Nijinsky separated.' Back at Ballydoyle, Liam Ward might have shuddered, as if someone had walked over his grave. 'Jocking-off' was the constant fear of every jockey lucky enough to be associated with a big race winner. And when the prime candidate was Lester Piggott, sentiment had little part to play.

But O'Brien was, and is, truly a man of his word. The arrangement was that Ward should have the rides in Ireland, Piggott elsewhere. And the next engagement for the wonder colt was the Irish Sweeps Derby at the Curragh.

Claude Duval reveals how Piggott, by now fully appraised of Nijinsky's incredible powers, tried to strike a private deal with Liam Ward to get the Irish Derby ride. Ward was amused by Piggott's optimistic effrontery but had no trouble in declining the offer. Piggott merely shrugged and said, 'See you at the Curragh, then.'

'But if I'm riding Nijinsky, why are you coming over?' asked Ward.

'I shall be second,' said Piggott.

And he was.

Piggott's mount, Meadowville, proved to be a very good, gutsy colt, but Nijinsky came from a different planet. The Irish bookmaking fraternity had no intention of aping their brothers across the water and started Nijinsky at a crucifying 4/11. There weren't many takers, but the spectators at the Curragh that afternoon hadn't really come to make their fortunes, merely to witness in the flesh the greatest racehorse of the generation. Throughout the whole mile-and-a-half gallop, Nijinsky stayed on the bit and Ward sat as still as a church mouse. Still the margin of victory was three lengths. Said Ward afterwards: 'My grandmother could have won on him today.' The victory took the colt's earnings to £170,000. Engelhard's costly investment had been repaid three times over.

But money was of little concern to the American where Nijinsky was concerned. As a devoted admirer of the great Ribot, which had retired unbeaten, Engelhard was determined that his colt should be the same. Stud valuation was part of it, I suppose – he said at the time, 'I am especially keen he should go to stud with an unbeaten record' – but I prefer to believe that it was Nijinsky's place in history which concerned him more.

In a curious way the ease of Nijinsky's win in the Irish Derby began to raise question marks about the quality of the three-year-old opposition in 1970. It is an old story, when one rival so dominates the rest. But O'Brien and Piggott were soon to have an opportunity to prove the colt's worth against older horses in the King George VI and Queen Elizabeth Stakes at Royal Ascot.

Since its inception in 1952 as part of the Festival of Britain, and at that time the richest horse race in Europe, the King George has grown in prestige until many would now regard it as one of only four significant middle-distance races in Europe, the others being the Epsom Derby, the Irish Derby and the Prix de l'Arc de Triomphe. Taking on Nijinsky at Ascot would be the previous year's Derby winner, Blakeney, French Oaks winner Crepellana, Karabas (Lester's winning ride in the Washington International), Italian Derby winner Hogarth and Coronation Cup hero Caliban.

When Nijinsky appeared in the parade ring, there were gasps of admiration from the huge crowd. Seldom can a racehorse have looked more the part than the wonder colt that day. His coat positively gleamed in the sunshine. There was nothing to touch him in either looks or conformation. This truly was Nijinsky's finest hour.

Lester Piggott, conscious of the quality of the opposition, needed to be at his most tactically astute. But, as usual, he kept his mount well covered up – though never seriously off the pace – until the final two furlongs before unleashing that devastating turn of speed. The distance over Blakeney was two lengths.

That the animal had responded so readily and in such devastating style says as much for its temperament as its talent. Here was an animal in the very prime of its racing life, fit and ready to run until it burst. Afterwards, O'Brien was ecstatic. So was Engelhard, and even Lester, now fully recovered from his dreadful wasting experience, was able to raise a smile or two. 'He's the best I've ridden,' said the champion jockey afterwards, and few who had seen Nijinsky that day could doubt the assessment.

Mind you, it wasn't an easy remark for Lester Piggott to make. Sir Ivor's blistering response to his urgings in the 1968 Derby, and later in the Washington International, was etched deeply in the jockey's memory. And there is no question that Piggott and Sir Ivor had an affinity that Piggott and Nijinsky could never quite match. Maybe that was because the horse didn't seem to need a rider as much as the rider needed the horse. You got the impression that the animal only required someone to sit on its back for it to qualify for another victory march. It was so intelligent, so profoundly talented, it needed little outside help.

The next question – the obvious one – was, where did Nijinsky go from there? Engelhard was determined that his colt should retire undefeated and had already arranged for the horse to stand at Clairborne, Kentucky, with a stud valuation of two and a quarter million pounds. An attempt was made to form a syndicate to keep the animal in Europe but, sadly, it failed.

O'Brien's target, not unnaturally, was the Arc, a race he viewed with affection as well as respect, bearing in mind the stunning victory of Ballymoss with Scobie Breasley aboard in 1958. But in the racing press a campaign was growing to enter Nijinsky for the St Leger, the final leg of the fabled Triple Crown. Richard Baerlein of the *Guardian* was one of the more vocal advocates. Writing in July, he said:

> My one regret with Nijinsky is that his connections have decided at this early stage not to run him in the St Leger. There is something special about a Triple Crown winner and we've not had one for 35 years. In 1935, Barham earned his crown without any undue exertion. It was saved to leave his mark as a stallion on the racing world. I am sure Nijinsky could earn the Triple Crown with even less difficulty than Barham unless the ground at Doncaster came up really heavy, as in Provoke's year in 1965 [a 28/1 outsider, trained by Dick Hern, ridden by Joe Mercer]. If it was heavy, then

Nijinsky could be withdrawn but the decision against running him in the St Leger has apparently been taken and, equally apparently, is irrevocable. The best news I could hear from Vincent O'Brien and his camp is a change of plan over the St Leger.

Talking to Baerlein at his Sussex home, we recalled that article and its significance in starting the campaign rolling.

'Vincent admitted to me later that articles of that kind must have had some influence over the decision making because they are written in the best interests of the horse in most instances. No owner these days likes to ignore entirely the view expressed in the English press. Some went further than I. So it really was the press campaign that caused him to run in that race.' And then, with an ironic chuckle, 'Of course, otherwise he'd have won the Arc . . .'

The point is that everyone got swept along by Nijinsky fever, including his ebullient owner. A week after returning to Ballydoyle, O'Brien got the call from Engelhard's racing manager, David McCall: 'Do you think you could get him ready in time for the Leger?'

O'Brien was in a dilemma. He had been aiming his colt towards Longchamp and while it would certainly need a prep race before then, he hardly felt the Doncaster classic – a quarter of a mile further – would provide it.

Set against that was the fact that the Leger had lost much of its prestige in recent years. It was unlikely to provide a horse of Nijinsky's calibre with any true opposition, so the only questions that mattered were: Would the ground be right? And would Nijinsky be fit? It was the second question that now worried O'Brien.

Five days after the King George triumph, Nijinsky was to suffer the only serious setback in his young life. A particularly virulent form of ringworm struck him down with such ferocity that most of his hair fell out. Ringworm is not an uncommon complaint in horses, but it is unpleasant and, in the case of a racehorse in training, somewhat limiting. It is simply not possible to put a saddle on the animal's back, let alone a rider, until the condition has healed. Nijinsky's lads reveal in Ivor Herbert's book, 'Even in late August you could not ride him for 10 minutes or he'd bleed.'

It all made training a matter of patience, and patience alone. There was no question of Nijinsky being tuned up on the gallops, so O'Brien would be forced to rely on the horse's natural talent and ability to get fit once the condition had passed. It left little time.

Word of the animal's illness did not make any significant impression in the English racing press or cause a ripple in the betting market. The security at Ballydoyle, both outside and inside, is tight, and aside from the trainer's official statements no one is likely to find out much about the condition of the animals there unless invited by O'Brien himself. So when Nijinsky finally reappeared on the racetrack at Doncaster in September, many of the British writers were seeing him for the first time since Ascot. And what they saw shocked them.

For while the animal certainly seemed to be on its toes, its coat was in a poor state – the most vivid contrast to Ascot. In fact one flank remained almost bald and there were one or two pundits, appraised earlier of the colt's condition, who questioned the wisdom of bringing it back so soon.

Lester Piggott was sure he could win, but he too harboured nagging doubts about the colt's tuning. 'I wondered whether he might not be a little over the top,' said the jockey later. But over the top or not, the result went exactly as predicted. Nijinsky was never off the bit and was comfortably in the lead one and a half furlongs from home. Johnny Seagrave on Meadowville – this time a 20/1 outsider – tried to conjure some magic out of his game animal, but although he got to within a length of Nijinsky at the finish, he never seemed likely to catch him. Said Lester afterwards: 'I never had a single anxious moment.'

O'Brien said little at the time but was to admit years later, 'The opposition may not have been strong but they certainly set out to make it a test of stamina. He won, but I wouldn't say he would have pulled out any more.' That was the view of many racegoers at the time. Nijinsky did enough – but where was that sparkle?

There was worse to follow. This time, the animal lost

weight on the trip back to Ireland – no less than 29 lb. A fit horse does not lose weight on that scale. Clearly Nijinsky was lacking something and O'Brien knew he was going to have the devil's own job getting him back into trim for the Arc. He was confident enough in the animal's ability to regain full fitness, but worried about the timescale.

After a while, the horse began to eat up again and was soon showing his old zest for work on the gallops. Even his coat was regaining its healthy sheen, and so pleased was the trainer with Nijinsky's progress that ten days before the big race he telephoned Lester in Newmarket to give him a progress report.

They chatted amiably but then O'Brien, giving voice to a private, nagging doubt he had always held about Longchamp, brought up the subject of riding tactics. The record shows, pointed out O'Brien, that the winner of the Arc usually holds a prominent position throughout the race. 'You must lie up,' he said. 'Few horses further back than fourth turning into the straight go on to win.'

The conversation, as Ivor Herbert reports it, is important in the light of what was to follow and the arguments the race was to fuel. 'Vincent now says, "So I made that suggestion about riding the horse . . . that he might not want to be too far out of his ground, turning into the straight – principally because of beaten horses coming back on him. Lester's exact reply to me was, 'I don't care if there are one hundred horses in front of me!' " '

If Vincent O'Brien had not been brooding so deeply on the fabulous animal in his yard as it prepared for the ultimate test, he might have taken Lester's remark in a normal, cheerful context. It was not, after all, a declaration of riding tactics, merely an expression of happy confidence. But O'Brien was scared that his jockey had *too* much respect for the animal's ability and too little for the opposition, which would again include Blakeney, Gyr and an out-and-out stayer called Sassafras. The French colt, trained by Philippe Mathet specifically for this target, would have the French star Yves St Martin aboard.

British and Irish punters seemed to share Piggott's

optimism. It was like Dunkirk in reverse as they squeezed into car ferries, BEA jets or private aeroplanes on a massive cross-Channel excursion. The elegant tree-lined Longchamp had never seen anything like it. On the other hand, it had never seen anything like the antics of the French press either as they laid siege to Nijinsky in the paddock. Lester sat aboard motionless as ever, but the animal was clearly upset by the jostling and constant popping of flash bulbs. It was an ill omen.

There was soon another. Nijinsky would go to post drawn on the outside, a position which severely limited the jockey's options. Not that Lester had planned to shoot Nijinsky to the front exactly. He would play his usual waiting game, only this time he would play it from further back, and indeed in the early stages of the race he had only three horses behind him. It was nail-biting stuff for O'Brien. 'He's too far out of his ground,' the Irishman kept repeating to himself as Blakeney and Sassafras began to take it up rounding the turn into the short home straight.

Sure enough, Nijinsky did seem well off the pace and, what was worse, he didn't seem to be getting any sort of opening to launch a run. He kept coming wider and wider on the outside while Sassafras appeared to be making his best way home on the rails. Yet for all his problems, Nijinsky managed to keep coming. As Geoff Lewis and Blakeney ran out of steam, Nijinsky was suddenly upsides of Sassafras with 150 yards to go. It seemed a formality to the British contingent, used to seeing this superior animal winning just as he liked. But they weren't prepared for the tenacity of the French horse, nor the skill and drive of jockey St Martin, who was squeezing every last ounce out of Sassafras.

Nijinsky was battling but the gears seemed to be stuck. In desperation, Lester gave the colt a crack with the whip to try and conjure up that missing overdrive, but instead of responding the animal dived further to the left, leaving Sassafras a head to the good. And that's the way they finished. The post came just too soon for the Irish wonder horse and the Impossible Dream was suddenly gone in a puff of smoke.

O'Brien was inconsolable. Keeping as tight a rein on his

outward emotions as he could manage, he told the stunned press, 'He had a lot to do. I do not want to be critical but his move was a little late.' The jockey, desperately disappointed but unaware of the first grey clouds of criticism that were building up around him, was forced to shrug it off as, 'Just one of those things. The draw meant I was not able to ride the kind of race I wanted to but I was quite happy, until the final two furlongs. He did swerve to the left when I hit him. I suppose he was tired.'

Next day, the storm clouds broke, and not just in the American press where Piggott was a favourite target for ill-informed rage. The British papers also blamed the jockey for leaving Nijinsky with too much to do. The *Guardian* stated sharply, 'Not only did he delay his challenge, but he came wide.' The *Sun* said, 'I really do think he left Nijinsky a hell of a lot to do.' The *Sporting Life* echoed O'Brien's earlier fears. 'He rode with over confidence,' it stated flatly.

The verdict had been so narrow, so many small factors may have contributed, that the sense of loss and disappointment was profound. A flop could have been shrugged off. But this . . . this hurt.

Later accounts would offer a more sober judgement than the first clarion call. The *Evening Standard*'s Chris Poole would state that a study of the film exonerates Piggott from all blame. The horse was in a position to win if he had been good enough, is the conclusion. And Roger Mortimer agrees.

The immediate reaction was to blame Piggott for leaving Nijinsky with too much to do. A cool and careful examination of the film, however, showed that Nijinsky had three lengths to make up on Sassafras when he launched his challenge. With a hundred and fifty yards to go he drew level and must have won had he maintained his effort. That, however, he failed to do. He faltered, and when Piggott applied his whip with his right hand, he veered to the left. Nijinsky had every chance but when the vital moment came he was unable to seize his opportunity. It was certainly not Piggott's fault that he lost.

Winning jockey Yves St Martin told the press, 'I looked back for Nijinsky and when I saw him move up beside me I thought I would be second. Then I felt that Nijinsky was in difficulties and I noticed that he was veering to the left. I called on Sassafras for a final effort and we made it.'

In the hands of a less sensitive jockey, Sassafras might *not* have made that effort and Nijinsky would have probably done enough. Equally, had the Irish horse been fully fit, and not distressed by the pre-race antics of the cameramen, would Sassafras have even been in at the finish? I doubt it. But one final point made by Ivor Bailey in his book *Champion Jockey*, published in 1972, intrigues me. He writes: 'Did Piggott approach the whole task in a mood of over-confidence with the idea of pouncing to win on the post to exact every ounce of drama out of a hairline victory?' And, most tellingly of all: 'Would Liam Ward, who understood the colt and had never been beaten on him, have adopted more orthodox tactics so that, with less to do in this finishing burst, he might have held off the rapidly tiring Sassafras?'

Of course, we shall never know for sure, but it is interesting to note that O'Brien still sticks by the original verdict he gave to American racing writer, Leon Rasmussen, five months after the race. 'I sincerely believe that the run Lester asked Nijinsky to make was over too long a distance . . . that, in the Arc, was an impossibility. The horse had shown Lester such tremendous speed in all his races that he felt he could pick him up whenever he wanted. Once again, Longchamp is different . . . '

Claude Duval, who in preparing his story about Piggott in the early seventies became close to Keith Piggott, quotes Lester's father as saying: 'I saw Lester and I could see how disappointed he was. I thought that he should have won. Lester looked at me knowingly and said, "I know. I had a great chance to go over to the rails at one point in the straight. I could have done it but I was frightened that the French stewards would have done me."'

If Lester felt that way, he clearly had little choice but to bring Nijinsky wide on that long run after Sassafras, and there is no doubt at all that he has had more than his fair share of suspensions in France. One does occasionally get the impression they are gunning for him.

For Charles Engelhard, defeat came hardest of all. Of course, the value of his stallion could not be disturbed – the stud syndicate had long since been settled at over two and a quarter million pounds – but he had always wanted Nijinsky to retire with an unbeaten record, like the great Ribot. That hope having vanished, he began to rake through the ashes of the disaster for a possible consolation. And he found it in the form of the Champion Stakes at Newmarket in October. Unbeaten he might not be, but still Nijinsky could go out in a blaze of glory.

O'Brien agreed to the proposal. He too felt they owed Nijinsky a chance to redeem his reputation. But when the colt returned to Ballydoyle he again lost weight – 11 lb this time – and it was clear to the trainer that this new engagement would be the biggest gamble of all.

O'Brien says now, 'Of course we wouldn't have gone for the Champion Stakes if he'd won the Arc, but he seemed all right after the race. He hadn't lost too much weight. The opposition seemed weak. It looked as if he had little to beat.'

Lester Piggott expressed no reservations and so once more the globe-trotting colt was shipped across the Irish Sea to Newmarket where it had all begun in such spectacular style one summer and one lifetime ago. And O'Brien was right about the opposition. It was indeed moderate with the battling five-year-old Lorenzacio, trained by Noel Murless, probably the pick of the bunch.

Lester knew all about Lorenzacio. Three times he had partnered the gutsy animal to victory that year, twice in France, once in England, and although this time Murless's jockey-in-waiting Geoff Lewis would get the ride, Piggott would not have swopped mounts at any price.

In the paddock, all seemed well. Nijinsky again looked in the peak of condition and his jockey seemed as imperturbable as ever. But as they moved on to the racecourse for the start, the crowd seemed to break ranks and crowd round their favourite. At one point, the suddenly troubled animal actually reared up on his hind legs – something he hadn't done since he was a two-year-old. And as they went to the post, Murless remarked to the groundsman standing near him that the horse was actually trembling. 'He can never win in that state,' declared the trainer.

Finally they were off, with Lewis making all the running on Lorenzacio, determined to blunt that legendary finishing speed by the most searching of gallops. Lester made a race of it, keeping Nijinsky well in touch so that coming into the final furlong the colt was in a position to win if he could quicken. And this time, he couldn't.

Lewis kept driving the big chestnut onward and Nijinsky could find nothing. Lorenzacio flashed past the winning post one and a half lengths to the good and the 100/7 outsider was suddenly the toast of Newmarket. Lester was philosophical. 'He was in a real state by the start of the race and at halfway I did not think we would be in the first three.' But then he added for posterity, 'He is still the best horse I have ever ridden.'

So ended the racing career of the most talked-about champion in the history of the turf. Not with a bang, but not quite with a whimper either because at least the courageous animal had given of his best on the day and second place was surely no disgrace.

Vincent O'Brien will always look back on that day as the most wretched of his life. 'I saw on the film afterwards that he was a sorry sight,' he told Ivor Herbert. 'It was a sad day. Really dreadful.' But like Lester Piggott he could still declare that, of all the many great animals he had been involved with, Nijinsky was the most brilliant. Again, like Lester, he will argue that Sir Ivor was 'the toughest' and that in the final analysis you would have to take a pin to separate them, but in the public mind there will never be any doubt. Nijinsky was a superstar. A horse that moved their emotions in a way that it never quite moved its jockey. For in the intervening years, Lester has sometimes switched positions and declared a preference for Sir Ivor when listing his canon of the great ones.

Richard Baerlein, whose subsequent book *Nijinsky: Triple Crown Champion* did much to fuel the legend, offers a more pragmatic view of Piggott's apparent volte-face.

I know Lester said in an *Express* interview five years later that Sir Ivor was the best horse he had ever ridden, but this was certainly contrary to his belief at the time and I much prefer to believe his earlier statement. It's the same with all these things, you tend to go by the opinion of the last person you have spoken to. The fact is that, having accomplished the Triple Crown, Nijinsky should never have run again. He would then have been rated in a far higher category like all these horses, Ribot, Sea Bird II. . . It was the same with Shergar. If he hadn't run in the St Leger.

The reason that he lost the Arc was that he was over the top and, in hindsight, that is exactly what Vincent O'Brien said. But they go on arguing about the draw and this and that. Is the draw going to be an excuse for any horse defeated in that race? It's nonsense. To me, the luck of the race and ability of the rider decides the issue, not the draw. Nijinsky was one of the best Derby winners ever but it lost its reputation by going on running. Engelhard summed it up best, 'We asked too much of our horse.'

14 | *Roberto*

Controversy has stalked Lester Piggott all his life, flitting in and out of the shadows like an alley cat. In 1970, he was a national hero – the man who rode Nijinsky: in 1972 he was public enemy number one – the man who 'stole' the ride on Roberto. Between the two contrasting events lay an obstacle course of if's and maybe's that would lead from Newmarket to Ballydoyle and finally, on the very eve of the 1972 Derby, to Epsom itself.

The catalyst for this improbable chain of events was a horse called Crowned Prince. As a yearling the full brother to Kentucky Derby winner Majestic Prince had cost a world record 500,000 dollars at Keeneland Sales in 1970 and had immediately been shipped to the Stanley House yard of Bernard van Cutsem in Newmarket. Van Cutsem was considered something of a genius at bringing on two-year-olds and when Crowned Prince appeared on the racecourse for the first time in August 1971, his high reputation seemed amply justified. The colt looked magnificent and the sight of the imperious figure of Lester Piggott astride its back was the jewel in the crown. Such was the interest in the animal that the stands at Newmarket were packed with racegoers; Crowned Prince was 2/7 on the books.

He ran like a champion too – at first. As the field of young hopefuls thundered down the straight to the two furlong marker, Lester seemed in total command. Then suddenly, inexplicably, he was going backwards. He finally finished well down the nineteen-runner field and Piggott and van Cutsem were left with nothing but a handful of puzzled explanations for the stunned press. Lester thought the horse simply ran green and would benefit from the outing. Van Cutsem shrugged and agreed, and then announced he would run Crowned Prince in blinkers on his second outing in the Champagne Stakes at Doncaster.

The ploy worked. Crowned Prince slaughtered his rivals, going away from the field a long way from home and even being eased up on the run-in as Rheingold chased into second place. Honour was restored. The wonder colt had come through, and, sure enough, Crowned Prince and Lester worked their magic on the crowds once more when it was announced that his next engagement would be the Dewhurst Stakes at Newmarket. Claude Duval wrote in the *Sun*: 'As I drove up from London, I had the feeling that nearly every car was heading towards the course to see this remarkable two-year-old and that equally remarkable 35-year-old Lester Piggott. People realized that Piggott's classic programme seemed to revolve around Crowned Prince and they were not going to miss any development.'

This time the huge crowd was not disappointed. Lester gave Crowned Prince a different ride from Doncaster, tucking him in to the centre of the field and then delivering his challenge inside the final furlong. The victory was an easy one. Crowned Prince, it seemed, could win any way you liked. The bookmaking fraternity were quick to react to this confident display and installed the colt at 5/2 for the 2,000 Guineas and 4/1 for the Derby. There were still plenty of takers, he seemed such a cert.

So Lester had much to comfort and warm him in the winter of 1971-2. Not only had he collected his eighth successive champion jockey's title but he had sneaked in to the year of Mill Reef and Brigadier Gerard for a classic bonus on Athens Wood in the St Leger. Neither of the superstars had elected to run and Lester only inherited the ride from Greville Starkey when that jockey was called on by Henry Cecil's stable. There was also the small matter of the St Leger providing one of the most vivid displays of riding skill Lester had

ever given. He rode a catch-me-if-you-can race, going out to
the front almost from the off, and one by one they tried. First
Alderney, then Homeric and finally Falkland, and it was
only the driving, pounding strength of Piggott and Athens
Wood that kept the duo a head in front at the line. Homeric
finished a neck ahead of Falkland.

And so on to Ireland and Ballydoyle where Vincent
O'Brien was doing his best to shut out the clarion call for
Crowned Prince echoing across the Irish Sea and, instead,
going quietly about preparing his own 1972 Derby hopefuls,
Boucher, Manitoulin and Roberto. He had a fancy for all
three but Roberto seemed the most talented, despite a streak
of laziness that caused the colt to stop working as soon as
he'd got his nose in front of the opposition. Lester came over
in the spring to run the rule over the trio, although by now he
was heavily committed to the brilliant Crowned Prince.
O'Brien recalls Lester showing a preference for Manitoulin
and no apparent enthusiasm for Roberto. 'That horse won't
win at Epsom,' he told the trainer after Roberto had
demonstrated his stop-go tactics in a training spin.

And yet . . . there must have been something about the
colt, for shortly afterwards Lester was quizzing O'Brien on
Roberto's general background and was thoughtful when
O'Brien remarked casually that Roberto always worked that
way. Perhaps he was making a mental note of possible second and third choices if the Crowned Prince project did not
work out. Not that there seemed much prospect of that as the
wonder horse came out for his three-year-old debut in the
Craven Stakes at Newmarket, once again gleaming in his
coat and trained to the minute.

Van Cutsem was confident. Lester was confident. But
halfway through the race, Crowned Prince seemed to lose all
appetite for the battle, just as he had on his two-year-old
debut, and it was all the jockey could do to hold him together
for a dismal fourth place. The public was dismayed, the
bookmakers puzzled. At Stanley House, the alarm bells were
clanging with a vengeance. Van Cutsem was used to juveniles
having an off day but not three-year-olds, and certainly not
Derby favourites. He asked Lester to give Crowned Prince a

thorough work-out on Yarmouth racecourse shortly after the Newmarket débâcle, and suddenly his worst fears were confirmed. The colt had a soft palette. The diamond was paste and a brilliant racing career was suddenly at a heartbreaking end.

So what now? Back to Ballydoyle and another work-out with the O'Brien hopefuls. The difference this time, however, was that only two of the candidates were still in the running, at least as far as Lester was concerned. Australian Bill Williamson – 'Weary Willie' to one and all in racing – had bagged Roberto, and even the talented Boucher was being talked of as a more likely St Leger than Derby candidate. So, it was Manitoulin or nothing. Lester accepted his fate stoically.

When news of Crowned Prince's failure broke, the Derby betting market was thrown into turmoil. Roberto was installed at the head of the field as the best of a bad bunch, while Lester's mount attracted little betting attention, despite the assistance of the champion jockey. But then, with Lester you never knew. As arch-rival Geoff Lewis wrote in a ghosted newspaper column in the *Daily Mail*, 'If Lester fell down a drain he'd come up with a white tie on.' A prophetic judgement if ever there was one.

Ten days before the Derby, Bill Williamson suffered a crashing fall at Kempton Park and returned to the weighing room with a painfully bruised shoulder. It was not a serious injury in any clinical sense but it was worrying for the trainer of the Derby favourite. O'Brien called Williamson for reassurance and swiftly got it. The jockey had been treated at once by Bill Tucker, a legend among professional sportsmen, and was told that proper rest would cure the problem within a week. O'Brien passed on the good news to John Galbreath, Roberto's millionaire owner and breeder. The American, however, was sceptical. He knew all about the stresses and strains of sport at the highest level; he owned the newly crowned world baseball champions, the Pittsburgh Pirates, and was as familiar with the treatment room as with the best seat in the grandstand. He wanted more than reassurance, he wanted proof.

Perhaps, too, Galbreath was beginning to entertain doubts about his jockey's ability to get the best out of Roberto. The Australian had had the ride in the 2,000 Guineas, and while the ground was all against the colt – muddy and clinging in vast patches – Williamson had not ridden one of his better races. Perhaps he nursed the colt too tenderly in the early stages, mindful of O'Brien's concern for the horse's knees in yielding conditions, but in any case he left Roberto a veritable mountain to climb as he headed after High Top inside the final furlong. High Top was a true stayer and while Roberto's impressive last-ditch acceleration got him to within half a length of the leader, the winning post beat them both. Afterwards, Williamson lamented, 'I'd have won the race if I'd known the horse better. I hung too far out.'

Lester, who had been forced to watch all this in a frustratingly detached way some distance back on a thoroughly indifferent animal, could only agree with the Australian's assessment. As soon as the race was over he sought out O'Brien. 'If I'd ridden that horse, I'd have won,' he told the trainer, and promptly offered his services for Roberto's next ride – the Derby! O'Brien recalls the incident with great good humour. It was typical Piggott. The offer was, of course, firmly declined. Williamson was booked and that was that. But then came that fall and suddenly everything was in the balance once more.

Three days before the race, Williamson again presented himself at Tucker's Mayfair clinic. The doctor was delighted with his progress. 'I don't see any reason why you shouldn't be able to ride,' he told the jockey. Again the news was passed to Galbreath and again the owner was sceptical. Seven days out of the saddle seemed entirely too long for his taste, but when it was learned that Williamson was to ride work for an Epsom trainer on the morning before the race, he agreed to postpone any firm decision until the fitness test was over. If only Weary Willie had known how close he was to losing the ride he might have taken more care in setting his alarm clock. As it was, he overslept, missed riding work and catapulted Lester into the saddle.

The saga that followed was pure pantomime, with O'Brien and Piggott cast as Hiss and Boo the villains. As for Galbreath, he should really have been given the part of Fairy Godmother, for while it was true that he had taken the final decision to replace Williamson (endorsed by O'Brien) he also promised the disappointed jockey the same prize as Piggott if Roberto won. At 7½ per cent that worked out at a consoling £6,000. No wonder Williamson kept his counsel as the war of words raged in the press. The most he would say was, 'Roberto is the form horse. I think he will win.' As for Lester, his comment was a priceless, 'This has all come as a complete surprise to me.'

Whatever the rights and wrongs of the affair – and most of the rights, in my view, belonged on the side of the owner – 6 June 1972 can be marked down as a watershed of sorts in the 'jocking-off' syndrome. From that day onwards, no jockey could feel entirely safe if Piggott wasn't actually nailed to his nominated mount and led handcuffed to the start. His long shadow was everywhere. One newspaper caught the humour of the situation neatly in a cartoon featuring two binocular-clad racegoers carefully examining a child's wooden rocking horse. The caption read: 'A rumour went round that he's the Derby favourite, now Lester insists on riding him. . .'

In fact, Bill Williamson was not the only jockey to lose his ride sensationally on Derby eve. The Scottish ace Duncan Keith was stood down by Irish trainer Paddy Prendergast after failing to appear for an early morning working gallop with his mount Gombos. Keith was somewhat less diplomatic than his Australian counterpart when he faced the press. 'This is disgraceful. Peter Walwyn, the trainer who has first claim on me, asked me to ride my Oaks mount Jakomina at Lambourn this morning. I tried to contact Mr Prendergast but failed. I have told him that I am bringing the matter up before the Epsom stewards. His decision was a great shock to me, and I feel very hurt because I have refused two other Derby mounts,' he wailed.

All this huffing and puffing and breastbeating provided Fleet Street with a marvellous running story, but there was still the small matter of the race itself to be won and by no means everyone was conceding it to Roberto. Yaroslav, with Mill Reef jockey Geoff Lewis on board, would have started 3/1 favourite until news of Lester's switch dropped him back a point. And Lyphard, narrowly beaten by Hard to Beat in the Prix Lupin, also became a lively candidate when Hard to Beat confirmed the form by going on to win the French Derby. Finally, there was Steel Pulse, saddled by jockey-turned-trainer Scobie Breasley who was showing the same silken touch with his animals as he had when riding them. Still, Lester at last had the ride he had always wanted, so in the final analysis it was up to him to make it stick. He so nearly didn't.

The problem proved to be an animal called Rheingold, American-bred, English-trained at the Lambourn stables of Barry Hills. Rheingold was one of those unpredictable characters who give trainers nightmares. His performance over the Epsom gradients in the Blue Riband Trial Stakes had suggested that he would be all at sea in the Derby, but he ran so impressively in winning the Dante Stakes at York that it seemed profligate to deny him his chance. Lester was only cautiously optimistic as they went down to the start.

If you run down through Derby history and freeze the moments that will live for ever, the finish of the 1972 classic will be one of them. It wasn't simply the tension of the neck-and-neck struggle inside the final furlong but the ferocity of the gladiatorial battle between Rheingold's Ernie Johnson and Roberto's Lester Piggott. Lester's whip cracked like a machine gun in the final 150 yards as he fought to keep Roberto running on with half a ton of Rheingold cannoning off his side. How he kept the animal balanced we will never know, but when the finish photograph was developed it showed Roberto a short head to the good. 'I didn't think I'd won,' said Lester, after enduring a twenty-minute wait for the verdict.

In fact Roberto had been battered and bumped all the way up the finishing straight. The pacemaker as they rounded Tattenham Corner, Pentland Firth, began to tie up badly in the final half-mile and it was a real struggle for his young jockey, Pat Eddery, to keep him straight. With Rheingold continually boring in on Roberto from the right it was inevitable that someone would get a bump, and first it was Roberto and then it was Pentland Firth. 'It didn't affect me more than a length,' said Eddery afterwards, adding, 'It was not Lester's fault. It happened because Rheingold bore in on Roberto.' Ernie Johnson, disappointed though he was in defeat, was equally quick to blame his own mount for any trouble. But he also thought he was an unlucky loser. 'I would have won on a galloping track,' he said, 'but Rheingold was hanging coming down the hill and I had to put my whip down at the distance, so badly was I going into Piggott.' So was Roberto only a winner because of the inspired driving of Lester that day? Most racing men seem to think so, but, ironically, one opinion that at least leaves the verdict open to debate comes from the winning trainer himself, Vincent O'Brien. 'It's impossible to say whether Williamson would have won,' he says, 'but I couldn't see it. Unless, that is, the horse would have done more for Williamson than he did for Piggott. Lester rode a great race on him. He did nothing wrong. But he told me afterwards that Roberto wasn't doing much for him, he should have won much more easily. . .'

In any event, the crowd were in no doubt about where their sympathies lay. When Lester finally led Roberto into the winner's enclosure he encountered an atmosphere so hostile it was almost tangible. Jeers and catcalls had already echoed around the stands when O'Brien and Galbreath were spotted chatting in the paddock and, indeed, two irate female racegoers attacked the trainer – one verbally, the other with her umbrella. The British may like to think they are the most sporting nation on earth, but they are not. Instead, they are obsessed with supporting the underdog – which is far from the same thing. And so, when Bill Williamson brought home the winner of the next race, the cheers were loud enough to lift the roof of the grandstand.

It would be a bit pious to describe the Roberto controversy as a shoddy affair, but it certainly left a nasty aftertaste. Racing historian Roger Mortimer wrote feelingly: 'Most people judged Mr Galbreath's action to be unsportsmanlike to say the least and Piggott himself was criticized for accepting the mount in such circumstances. It was a common view that if owners are incapable of displaying loyalty to their jockeys, then they have not got the slightest right to expect loyalty in return and it is entirely their own fault if they fail to get it.' On the other hand, an entry in *Racehorses of 1972* puts the matter baldly in perspective: 'It's no use complaining about the demise of old fashioned values such as sportsmanship. Racing is now a business, like it or not; the difference between winning and losing the Derby nowadays could be well over a million pounds.'

That entry certainly puts the owners' case. But what of the jockeys? Says Willie Carson: 'There is a fair possibility that someone will be jocked-off in the Derby. He [Piggott] has the best record and that is why no one is safe when he goes hunting for a ride. It's a fact of life. The owners pay the bills and they are entitled to have who they want. I believe there is more to life that just one race. But Lester is something special and we have just got to put up with it. I wouldn't like to see anything changed.'

Scobie Breasley says: 'We all have to live with that kind of thing in the racing world. Getting jocked-off happens to every rider sooner or later and you could hardly blame Lester Piggott for taking the ride on Roberto when it was offered. Of course, Lester is a great man for the telephone, always likely to ring up an owner or trainer and offer himself for a fancied ride. But that's all part of getting to the top, especially when you're riding as a freelance.'

The last word, appropriately, belongs to Williamson, who tragically died in 1979. He said: 'Lester would have been foolish not to take the ride on Roberto when it was offered.'

Roger Mortimer's comment on loyalty was to be given vivid expression just a few weeks after the Derby when Roberto was entered for the prestige handicap race of the season, the Benson and Hedges Gold Cup at York. Piggott, naturally, was offered the ride. But he had also been approached by Barry Hills to partner Rheingold and he opted for the latter. 'Dog bites man' the headline might have run, and certainly the American was less than amused by Piggott's lack of loyalty. But, as always, Lester's decision was based on sound, unsentimental judgement. He merely considered Rheingold a better bet than Roberto over York's one and a quarter plus miles, although he also considered the unbeaten Brigadier Gerard a better bet still. That was a ride he couldn't beg, borrow or steal, however. It had been the province of Joe Mercer from day one and the younger brother of Manny had carried the Hislop colours to twelve successive victories, including the 1971 2,000 Guineas when Mill Reef had been mown down. The Brigadier needed one more win to pass Ribot's record twelve on the trot.

The main factor influencing Lester was Roberto's dismal performance in the Irish Derby, in which – another irony – Bill Williamson had ridden Steel Pulse to victory for Scobie Breasley. O'Brien's home jockey, Johnny Roe, had been given the mount and in O'Brien's opinion that was the crucial difference. Roberto knew Roe and Roe knew Roberto – they were too relaxed in each other's company, and as the Irish colt was basically very lazy, the combination was not exactly galvanic.

Timeform, however, had a different reason for Roberto's poor showing. Their correspondent had been horrified by Piggott's apparent whipping of Roberto to get up in the Derby and said '. . . we don't propose to look any further for an explanation of his defeat'. And yet, according to O'Brien, when he and owner Galbreath visited Roberto's stables afterwards they found not a mark on him. As Lester said, 'I was hardly able to hit him because I hadn't got any room!'

Galbreath confirmed that he was a man for the grand gesture when, instead of engaging any one of half a dozen top European jockeys, he sent to America for the Panamanian ace Barulio Baeza to ride Roberto at York. Even O'Brien was surprised, but unlike many of the insular pillars of British racing (then, not now) he knew Baeza by reputation, and, furthermore, he had seen enough of the day-to-day grind of the American dirt-track scene to know that anyone who rose to the top in that pressure cooker had to be very good indeed. And Baeza was. He was also cocky, a fact which would prove his downfall in races to come. But, for now, he was just the surprise package Roberto needed on its back if it was to let talent dictate over laziness.

Vincent O'Brien gave Baeza a thorough briefing on Roberto and his rivals, but in essence he admits he left the riding decisions to Baeza. The Panamanian needed no subtle tactical plan in any case. He knew only one way and that was to shoot from the stalls like a bullet and kick your way home as fast as you can. That's what he did, all right. He was so fast he shattered the York course record, and Mrs Hislop, owner of Brigadier Gerard, exclaimed in astonishment, 'Roberto ran as if he'd been stung by a bee.' Lester and Rheingold were never in the picture, in fact everything in the race – barring Brigadier Gerard – was off the bit and struggling before the field had even entered the straight. Baeza just kept Roberto flying and the unbeatable Brigadier couldn't even get to within a length of him. It is necessary to add that Roberto never ran quite like that again, despite the prompting of Baeza. In the Prix Niel, a prep race for the Arc, Baeza trailed Hard to Beat from gun to tape without ever looking like catching him. And in the Arc itself he tried a repeat of the York tactics to such ill effect that O'Brien was left apoplectic with rage.

Ivor Herbert, in his absorbing study of O'Brien's great horses, reveals that the great trainer is angered still. 'He thought he knew how to ride Longchamp after the Prix Niel. There was no question of having a discussion, of taking advice! He had it all figured out. They went so fast that they did the first five furlongs in the same time it took to run the big French sprint, the Prix de l'Abbaye, that day. And they covered the first mile quicker than in the one mile Prix du Moulin also on that same day.' What made it doubly galling for O'Brien was that the other horse involved in that do-or-die gallop was his recent St Leger winner, Boucher, also in the hands of an American rider, Lafitte Pincay. Roberto trailed in seventh, which made him the first three-year-old home, though that was hardly compensation.

And there the Roberto story came pretty much to an end. He was kept in training as a four-year-old, but the magic had gone. Lester Piggott did ride him to victory in a sub-standard Coronation Cup at Epsom, but he was withdrawn from the

Eclipse when a thunderstorm soaked the Kempton track, and he ran badly in the King George VI and Queen Elizabeth Stakes, again with Lester aboard. Finally, he was withdrawn from the Benson and Hedges Gold Cup at York when the ground became heavy. A pulled ligament kept him out of the final engagement of his career, the Champion Stakes at Newmarket, and thereafter he was retired to a successful career at stud.

In a sense, the Roberto story and the Lester Piggott story only made a fleeting acquaintance, but on the occasions they were together, the sparks really flew and so it is no wonder that when people speak of Piggott's career highlights, the American colt is up there near the front. The same cannot be said of Boucher, but it was that animal that gave Lester an unprecedented fifth St Leger victory in six consecutive outings and provided ample compensation for his failure to retain his champion jockey title for the first time in nine years. Only six animals opposed the O'Brien colt in that race, none very highly regarded, and even the most one-eyed Lester supporters were forced to admit that the Great Man had a huge slice of luck on that day.

To begin with, Boucher refused to leave the stalls when the starter's flag went up. Fully five seconds elapsed before Lester was able to coax him out of the gate, and if the field had gone at anything like a normal pace, he would have been left for dead there and then. As it was, they proceeded as if part of a funeral cortège and a disbelieving Piggott found himself back in contention before they had gone half a mile. Then, coming into the home straight, Boucher became totally unbalanced as he challenged the leader, Our Mirage, and only the swift transference of his whip from one hand to the other prevented Boucher from barging Jimmy Lindley's colt and incurring a certain disqualification. Fortunately, there was enough straight left for Lester to regain control and after that Boucher's superior class was made to tell. The official distance was three lengths and half a length with Ginevra third.

At season's end the final tally showed that Lester had managed only 103 winning rides from a miserly 464 mounts, a sharp contrast indeed from 1971 when he had put up 162 winners from 630. But the inescapable fact was that times were changing, and not just because a new breed of super riders – headed by Willie Carson, seconded by Pat Eddery – had emerged to challenge his supremacy. Lester was tired of the chase. The physical toll of driving here and flying there just to notch another winner was at last beginning to pall. He had nothing left to prove in the championship race. It was the big winners he wanted now and Boucher had given him his twentieth classic. There on the horizon suddenly was Frank Buckle's overall record of twenty-seven. It was within his compass if somehow he could find a guaranteed supply line of high-class three-year-olds. It was a tall order but it was at that very moment as he contemplated the next development in his career that a puckish little man who had inherited millions from a pools empire in England began to contemplate *his*, and what he decided was that above all else he wanted to breed classic race winners.

The man was Robert Sangster and the third great phase in the Piggott legend was about to begin.

Epsom's twists and gradients and a patient Lester had driven Empery past Relkino in the finishing straight for a splendid three-lengths victory. That made it seven Derby wins — one more and he would have the record.

All the omens looked right when Lester cruised home by four lengths in the Larkspur Stakes at Leopardstown and then went on to record an equally impressive win at Newmarket in the Dewhurst. That race had the English press sitting up and taking notice for the first time, and *Timeform* would even go so far as to rate The Minstrel a heady 116 at the end of his debut season. His three-year-old career began with yet another win, this time in the mud of Ascot and the 2,000 Guineas Trial. The ground was so bad the field was unable to enter the stalls and was flag started, but it didn't worry The Minstrel.

Lester went to Newmarket convinced that he had solved his annual Derby equation. According to the bookmakers, the 2,000 Guineas would be a formality and, in fact, hopes were high in the O'Brien camp that they could pull off two classic wins because The Minstrel's unbeaten stable mate, Cloonara, was equally well supported for the 1,000 Guineas. Why everything went so horribly wrong is one of those mysteries that litter the history of horse-racing. The Minstrel was given every chance. Passing the Bushes, the distinctive white socks could be clearly seen as Piggott sought to deliver his challenge, but somehow, the accelerator pedal got stuck and Nebbiolo and Tachypous passed him inside the final furlong — and that was that. With Cloonara also failing to deliver the goods in the filly's classic, it was a disconsolate team that travelled back to Ireland to unravel what had gone wrong.

On the face of it there seemed to be nothing. The Minstrel travelled well, ate well and exercised with his usual bubbling enthusiasm, and Piggott needed little persuading from either Sangster or O'Brien to have another crack on him in the Irish 2,000. This was better. The Minstrel ran up much more to his form, yet it still wasn't good enough to oust Pampapaul in a frantic photo finish. Once again, there were long faces all round. But Lester had detected something in this perfor-

15 | The Great Triumvirate

Robert Sangster was restless, frustrated and perhaps a little bored as he sat in his palatial office contemplating the coming flat racing season. Horses were his passion, but his involvement with them was too peripheral. True, he owned a small stud and the blue, green and white Sangster silks were occasionally in evidence at his local Haydock Park course near Liverpool. But it wasn't nearly enough to satisfy a man used to operating on the grand scale.

As heir and managing director of the Vernon's Pools empire, Sangster was wealthy enough to paper his walls with pound notes should the fancy take him. But he was no dilettante. He was a born businessman who believed in making money, as well as people, work for a living. And he saw in racing a unique opportunity to create a profitable business out of an all-consuming hobby.

Once the idea had taken shape he cast around for advice. Living close by in Cheshire was the man who bore the most famous name in the turf, Lord Derby, and it was to that wise and experienced man that he took his enthusiasm. Lord Derby was intrigued, but he was aware of the pitfalls, the trip wires that lay in wait for the unwary and, crucially, the under-financed. His advice was simple and succinct. 'Find the best trainer, get the best advice, but be prepared to spend about a million pounds.' He might have added, 'Get the best jockey, too' but in 1974 that particular commodity – one Lester Keith Piggott – was doing very nicely thank you on his own account.

Sangster went away and thought about Lord Derby's words. Was it a gamble or was it a genuine business investment? He decided it was a business investment. Horses could become stock as surely as used cars or any other saleable commodity. Indeed, in 1975, he apparently sold Vernon's £8 million second-hand car investment and purchased horses instead. But by that time he had built the base of his pyramid with the firmest building blocks available – he had trainer Vincent O'Brien and breeder and bloodstock genius, John Magnier.

Between them, the Syndicate, as it was at once christened, would transform first the bloodstock and breeding industry and then the face of racing itself. In particular, they would return to England and Ireland so many of the best bloodlines lost to America. And finally, they would create the biggest racing empire the world has ever seen. To achieve all this in what amounts to a little under a decade required more money than you could shake a fist at – certainly a great deal more than Lord Derby's projected one million. But it was in the choice of backers for his syndicate that Sangster proved himself such a shrewd businessman.

Above all, the team needed luck and they hit the jackpot almost immediately with an animal whose name has passed into racing legend – The Minstrel. As Vincent O'Brien's wife Jacqueline told Ivor Herbert, 'It was like a win in the casino early in the night, so that you are playing for the rest of the evening with casino money. You can be more courageous.' And yet it was one bet the Syndicate nearly didn't lay. It finally came down to Lester Piggott.

Shortly after the Syndicate was formed, O'Brien was jetting off to America to run his thumb over the yearlings at the July Keeneland Sales. He was looking for another Nijinsky – who wasn't? – but instead he found himself mesmerized by an animal who was as far removed from that great animal in looks as it was possible to get. Instead of being a bay, this one

was a chestnut. Instead of being big, he was tiny. But damning of all, the yearling had four white socks. The racing jingle that goes: 'One buy, two try, three doubt go home without.' It has served many a trainer well ov years – white legs have often proved prone to infectio unsoundness. But still there was something about thi mal which kept O'Brien coming back for second look second look.

In the end, two factors clinched it for O'Brien. The was The Minstrel's pedigree – sire Northern Dancer, Fleur, daughter of Nijinsky's dam, Flaming Page. The ond was that he sweated up a lot and O'Brien took that a good sign in Northern Dancer colts. And finally, if c dence was any help in the matter, his breeder was Taylor who had started the ball rolling with Nijinsky.

So Robert Sangster found himself writing out his major cheque for a cool 200,000 dollars. Much larger would follow, of course, but for now it was enough tha Syndicate was off and running with what might – just m – turn out to be classic material. The Minstrel proved ea train, which was encouraging, but because of his size he a long time to come to hand and he didn't make his two-old racecourse debut until the early part of September in the Moy Stakes at the Curragh. He was ridden that Thomas Murphy and he won with such ease that h the six-furlong track record, virtually unopposed.

Now it was Lester's turn to put him through his pa by now firmly deposed champion jockey – Carson Eddery had divided the last three titles between th hungry for another Derby success. Since his brilli on Roberto in 1972 there had been a string of d ments, until out of a clear blue sky had come En remarkable animal, trained by the equally Egyptian-born, French-based Maurice Zilber, h the 1976 prize against every prediction but its tr Lester, in a ghosted newspaper column in the *dard*, had remarked that 'I'll need an elepha Wollow', the 2,000 Guineas winner and hottes ites. Fortunately, Wollow had proved incapa

mance that gave him a grain of comfort, and soon after weighing in he sent a message for Sangster and O'Brien to meet him in the changing room.

It was by now an open secret in racing circles that Lester had been courting the ride on Blushing Groom, a precociously fast animal owned by the Aga Khan and trained by François Mathet in France. But this year there was to be no jocking-off scandal. Both men were adamant that the ride should go to stable jockey Henri Samani despite his lack of Epsom experience. The fact is, Lester had very few places to go, although O'Brien did have two other runners, Be My Guest and Valinsky, which could not be ignored. Sangster and O'Brien paced the room. Should they or shouldn't they send The Minstrel to Epsom? Would he or wouldn't he get the full trip? Suddenly, a quiet voice from the corner of the room cut through the circular conversation.

'Look,' said Lester, 'if you run him, I'll ride him.' And that was that. The big bet that Jacqueline O'Brien had talked about had been finally laid. As Vincent O'Brien was to say afterwards, 'Lester doesn't say much but when he talks, you listen!' Lester's decision not only concentrated minds in that small, draughty changing room but changed the face of a complete racing season. To say nothing of making a fortune for the Syndicate.

Once it became known that Lester would pin his hopes on The Minstrel, the smart money began pouring in once again – and not just from the punters this time. On the eve of the race, the owners received a £1 million pound offer for the horse and, in turning it down, eventually enriched themselves to the tune of 4.5 million dollars. The general feeling, though, was that this was a sub-standard Derby field, although there was nothing sub-standard about the pulsating finish conjured by Lester Piggott and that Scottish dynamo Willie Carson.

The pace was a scorcher and as they came round Tattenham Corner it was obvious that only three animals were seriously left in the race – Carson's Hot Grove, The Minstrel and the favourite, Blushing Groom. Three furlongs from home, Carson kicked on and now only The Minstrel pre-

sented a challenge. It was here that that remarkable animal
showed the reserves of strength and courage that made him a
true champion. Piggott's whip whirled like a windmill as
they began to cut down the lead, but it was only inside the
last 150 yards that The Minstrel ranged up alongside before
stretching for victory on the line. The distance was a neck
and five lengths. 'Lester had to be hard on him,' said O'Brien
afterwards, recalling the pained expressions on many faces
as the jockey drove him to the line. 'He needed all his power
and skill. The Minstrel was very game.'

With the gamble safely landed, nothing could now disturb
the equilibrium of the season, though O'Brien was faced
with a dilemma in choosing between The Minstrel and
Alleged to represent his stable in the Irish Derby at the Curragh. Alleged, who had been brought to Ballydoyle as a two-
year-old after O'Brien had rejected him as a yearling, was
also being whispered of in the superstar class. Which should
be run? Eventually, the firmness of the ground decided him
in favour of The Minstrel, much to the disgust of Alleged's
part-owner Bob Fluor, who had flown over from America
with family, relatives and business partners to see him run.
Sangster had an equal share in both animals and it was he
who finally passed on the news, placating the furious owner
by offering him a cool one million pounds for his holding.
The offer was accepted, though Fluor did retain a 5 per cent
interest in the animal which would later pay handsome
dividends.

So The Minstrel it was who stepped into the spotlight on
the Curragh and, once again, with Lester driving him on, he
was a most handsome winner. There was a measure of controversy in this race too, because O'Brien's colt seemed
incapable of steering a straight line, and while the one and a
half lengths he finished ahead of Lucky Sovereign was
eloquent testimony to his superiority, there was just a suspicion of interference early on. The objection was overruled
and The Minstrel kept the race. In the final furlong, as Piggott brought him under the whip, the animal had veered so
far off a true course to the left of the field that he practically
ended up in the grandstand.

Next came Ascot and the narrowest of all The Minstrel's victories – about three inches, according to his trainer. This time Lester even came in for some criticism from O'Brien for striking the front too soon, but even though Orange Bay fought The Minstrel to the line and beyond, there seemed something inevitable about the final outcome. This King George win boosted the colt's earnings to a record £315,211, a handsome return on the 200,000 dollar purchase price, to say nothing of the four million plus syndication fee. With so much money riding on its soundness and reputation, it was no surprise when O'Brien announced the colt's retirement immediately after Ascot. 'He's done enough,' he said. Actually, The Minstrel did have one more race of sorts – with the US authorities as they sought to ban the import of all horses from Europe to avoid a plague of equine metritis.

Alleged's career overlapped The Minstrel's and so for a while he was quite overshadowed. But Lester was never in any doubt about the quality of the animal which would give him two of his most satisfying triumphs. If Alleged is not spoken of in the awe that attends great Derby winners like Sea Bird and Sir Ivor, it is because he flourished not at home but overseas, notably in France. There he is revered. After his second successive triumph in the 1978 Arc de Triomphe, and after four months off the racecourse, he was mobbed as enthusiastically as any pop or film star. Hairs were actually pulled from his tail and his mane as souvenirs – yet Alleged didn't bat an eyelid.

Those Arc wins, the first in 1977 over New Zealand's Balmerino, the second over Willie Shoemaker and Trillion, finally laid the ghost of Longchamp for Piggott. There had been so many near misses down the years, so much criticism for races it was claimed he should have won – the most famous being Nijinsky in 1970, I suppose, the most notorious on the brilliant filly Park Top the year previously. But now he had atoned fully, just as, in 1973, when he had steered Rheingold home ahead of Allez France, he had broken his duck.

The Sangster–O'Brien–Piggott partnership was to thrive as a unit for another three seasons, but while the wins continued to mount up and the money pour in by the truckload, after The Minstrel and Alleged there was suddenly a pause in the middle-distance production line. In fact, there were some very expensive flops and it was Lester's opinion of one of those flops, Monteverdi, that put the relationship under strain for the last time.

As a two-year-old Monteverdi had shown all the right credentials, winning the National Stakes trial in Ireland and, more important, the William Hill Dewhurst Stakes, which O'Brien has long regarded as the ideal try-out race for his classic hopefuls. Then in the Irish 2,000 Guineas the expensive colt flopped spectacularly. His connections were understandably dejected by the sudden loss of form, but Lester's scathing criticism of the colt was astonishing. In full earshot of the racing press he described Monteverdi as 'useless', which may have been true, but such a remark uttered in public is hardly likely to enhance an animal's valuation as a stallion. Sangster was far from pleased by the indiscretion, O'Brien was furious. But Lester is Lester and nothing was going to change his perception of his charted course. He was not one for the master-and-pupil relationship and it would be foolish to deny that he and O'Brien had been seeing matters rather differently in the months since Alleged's double triumph.

Within four months of the 'Monteverdi' incident, the Great Triumvirate was no more. It was announced quietly from Ballydoyle that Pat Eddery would be taking over from Lester Piggott as of the 1981 season. It was such a bombshell that at first no one could believe it. When the press tackled Lester all he would say, disarmingly, was that he was tired of all the travelling to and from Ballydoyle to ride work and would welcome a rest, as well as a change of pace. Well, of course, no one believed that; but before the rumour machine could get into full swing, Sangster, O'Brien and Piggott joined verbal forces to explain that it was a mutual parting of the ways, a chance to explore new ground for them all. There was no question of a sacking. And of course the tributes then began to pour like honey from the appropriate mouths.

The racing world, and public, may have been shocked, but those running on the inside track were anything but surprised. As soon as the Eddery appointment was made known it was announced that Lester would be filling the 'vacancy' at Warren Place to enable Joe Mercer to take over Eddery's former position at the Peter Walwyn stables. As Henry Cecil just happened to be the most successful trainer in the land at the time it was a handsome coincidence indeed!

It was inevitable that the Triumvirate should illuminate the heavens as briefly and as spectacularly as a comet. The personalities were so disparate: Piggott and O'Brien, geniuses both, were bound to clash eventually. Lester's dogmatism is legendary and, genius though he may be, he doesn't always make the right decisions. One horse that eluded his practised eye was the Barry Hills-trained (on behalf of Sangster) Hawaiian Sound, a bargain-basement buy at 32,000 dollars and one of the unluckiest animals of the decade. His big race near-misses would include the 1978 English and Irish Derbies, the King George VI and Queen Elizabeth Stakes and the Champion Stakes. Handsome compensation would come in the Benson and Hedges Gold Cup at York in August, but that victory would only underline the frustration for Lester as he considered what might have been.

Once again everything revolved around which horse Lester would partner in the Derby. In the spring of 1978 that looked like O'Brien's highly regarded Try My Best, but when that animal failed badly, Lester found himself scanning the horizon once more. Hills was convinced of Hawaiian Sound's ability and moved heaven and earth to try to persuade the jockey to take the ride. But Lester dithered and finally opted for another O'Brien colt, Inkerman – a dismal selection, as it turned out. Like many a trainer before him, Barry Hills had taken a Piggott wink to equal a nod, and when the refusal came it hit him hard. Sangster and Hills put heads together and decided on a bold course, to send for the top American (but veteran) jockey, Willie 'The Shoe' Shoemaker. He had, at forty-six, already ridden a world record 7,300 winners, but not in England. In fact he'd never even seen Epsom and his first sight of the switchback course on Derby morning had him gasping in surprise. His description of Tattenham Corner – 'It's like coming down a ski slope without skis' – was as apt as it was endearing. But it certainly didn't frighten him off.

Shoemaker conjured the most superb ride out of Hawaiian Sound. He rode the course like an old Epsom hand and it was only a desperate, driving finish by Greville Starkey on Shirley Heights that robbed him of the prize in the last stride. And Lester? He was twenty-first out of twenty-five.

Shoemaker was delighted when he was invited to renew his partnership with the Derby runner-up in the Irish equivalent at the Curragh. Again he rode well, but this time he found two too good for him, Shirley Heights and Exdirectory with Lester a close-up fourth on Inkerman. Before jetting back to America, the Shoe was booked for a third run on Hawaiian Sound in the King George VI and Queen Elizabeth Diamond Stakes (as it was now called following De Beers' sponsorship), a race which top racing journalist Chris Poole happily describes thus: 'It is doubtful whether a collection of better quality horseflesh has ever met to contest the principal mid-season prize in the English calendar.'

As Poole notes:

A total of nine current or former champion jockeys from five different countries had mounts in this exceptional race. Representing the host nation were Lester Piggott (Trillion), Pat Eddery (Exdirectory), and Willie Carson (Dunfermline), with Yves St Martin (Acamas), Freddie Head (Montocontour), Maurice Phillipperon (Guadanin), and Philippe Paquet (Rex Magna) forming a powerful presence. New Zealand champion Mark Campbell partnered Balmerino and, of course, Willie Shoemaker was on Hawaiian Sound. But, as any student of racing will vouch, there is nothing quite as unpredictable as the Turf, and this positive galaxy of big names were to lose out to a young jockey who appeared out of his depth in such illustrious company and who was riding a horse whose reputation in terms of international competition had yet to be established.

The youngster was John Reid who had accepted the first jockey retainer at Fulke Johnson Houghton's Blewbury stables on the understanding that the first-string horses would be ridden by Lester or Willie Carson whenever either was available. Reid accepted this willingly enough, but in this particular race both were otherwise engaged and Reid got the mount on the brilliant Nijinsky colt, Ile de Bourbon. The race lived up to its reputation and Reid made one for himself that day in his handling of the winner. Yves St Martin got the French Derby winner Acamas close, but not close enough, and Hawaiian Sound's late run could earn him no better than third place. Lester, again out of the frame, could only look on in frustration.

There was a sensational sequel to the race when a routine dope test found the prohibited substance salicylic acid in Acamas's urine and the horse was disqualified, thus promoting Hawaiian Sound to second. Fortunately, trainer Guy Bonaventure was cleared of any intent and fined a token £250. The horse's owner, meanwhile, Marcel Boussac, created shock waves of his own when his multi-million business empire collapsed with a crash that echoed round the world.

Willie the Shoe returned to the States a happy and well rewarded man. Now it was Lester's turn to take over Hawaiian Sound, which he did brilliantly in the Benson and Hedges Gold Cup. His 'told you so' expression as he led the colt into the winner's enclosure was reinforced by sarcasm when a delighted Robert Sangster asked the jockey what he might like as a 'present'. 'Just give me how much it cost to fly that Shoemaker over here twice,' he told the owner. If Sangster was hurt by the remark, he wasn't particularly offended. The fact that Lester had won, and won well, was enough. Sangster, although anything but a callous individual, is above all a pragmatist – and he had come to know his jockey very well indeed over the months. He might have pointed out that Lester had brought the Shoemaker experiment on himself by declining the Derby ride on Hawaiian Sound, and Lester, a pragmatist himself, would probably have agreed.

But, given the sensitive nature of the business Sangster, O'Brien and Piggott were in, it doesn't do to hang out your dirty washing in public. The following season would not improve Lester's classic tally, now standing at twenty-three and in very realistic range of Buckle's record twenty-seven. When Milford could manage only a modest Derby tenth and Monteverdi a wretched fourteenth, his classic drought had climbed up to a thirsty fourteen and, for the first time, anno domini was becoming a factor. By the end of 1980 Lester was forty-five.

Age was no factor as far as O'Brien and Sangster were concerned. They didn't have to ride the horses, but united as they were in recognizing Lester's genius and status as the number one jockey, they knew equally that there were other good ones about who could match their needs exactly. Pat Eddery, for example.

Since bursting onto the scene in 1969, Eddery had progressed from whip-brandishing firebrand to level-headed champion, taking the title for the first time in 1974 and holding it for four successive seasons until Willie Carson had claimed it back again. He was riding as brilliantly in 1980 as he had been in 1978, but his trainer Peter Walwyn was having wretched luck with his animals as the coughing virus attacked his stables again and again. The O'Brien–Sangster bid for his services, then, came at exactly the right time in his career, although the reported £120,000 retainer and fortieth share in any racehorse sold as a stallion was in any case beyond refusal. Yet such was Eddery's loyalty to the man who had first believed in him and shared so many years of success that a genuine tug of war ensued before he could be persuaded back across the Irish Sea. O'Brien and Sangster knew then that they had a jockey every bit as tough and single-minded as Lester Piggott, but perhaps one not so obsessively self-centred.

Brough Scott says of him: 'Lester has a touch of gipsy restlessness and hunger about him, and his incessant testing of other people's classic hopes had O'Brien saying as long ago as 1976, "I would like him to ride my horses in all the big races, but none in the trials or gallops, for he rides them to find things out for himself and not to suit me."'

Noel Murless discovered the same thing in the mid-sixties, but if either trainer had imagined that one day the 'hungry gipsy' would spear himself on his own fork, they were to be far wide of the mark, because, in addition to all his genius, Lester possesses a further quality that money just can't buy – luck! As he says himself with Micawber-like frankness, 'Something will turn up – it usually does.'

What turned up in 1981 was a spectacular change in his fortunes: a champion jockey title once more and two classic successes which would take him within touching distance of Buckle. Perhaps the break with O'Brien was the catalyst he required.

16 | *King of the Classics*

All eyes were on the pale, crumpled figure who lay in a welling pool of his own blood on the Epsom grass. His eyes were hodded and vacant, his breath came in short rasping gasps, but he was alive. That in itself seemed a miracle after the drama that thousands of racegoers had just witnessed as the animal in gate four had suddenly gone berserk.

Winsor Boy, a five-year-old from the Wiltshire stables of Bob Turnell at Ogbourne Maisey, was a sprinter of some ability but uncertain temperament. After years of darting out of the starting stalls like an arrow from a bow, the animal had inexplicably developed an aversion to the tiny metal cage with its padded gates, and as Lester led the horse towards his allotted place on that April afternoon, he sensed a fatal tenseness in the animal beneath him. 'Straight in, straight out', thought the jockey, hoping the manouevre would reassure the colt. But the exit gates wouldn't open and suddenly Winsor Boy was squealing and butting to escape from his prison. Finally, he bent down on his foreknees and wriggled out under the narrow gap at the bottom of the gate, 'scraping the unfortunate Piggott off his back like an old coat of paint', as Christopher Poole so chillingly described it.

The ambulance arrived and the semi-conscious jockey, his gaping head wound quickly dressed, was rushed to the

Epsom and District hospital for emergency treatment. It was discovered that his right ear had been partially severed and thirty-one stitches were needed to sew it back into place. Otherwise the injuries were superficial, bruising and lacerations. Most importantly, there was no sign of a brain injury.

The race had been televised and thousands were witness to the catastrophe. Small wonder that the hospital was besieged, not just by press and television crews but by members of the general public all anxious for news of the Great Man. 'I didn't know I was so popular,' said Lester as the fruit and the flowers and the telegrams began to mount up in his room. The immediate crisis was mercifully over, but there was the small matter of the 1,000 Guineas in a week's time in which Lester had been booked to ride the 6/4 favourite Fairy Footsteps for Henry Cecil. A hasty conference between trainer and jockey brought further reassurance. 'Lester assures me he will ride Fairy Footsteps at Newmarket and I am not even thinking about an alternative jockey,' said Cecil.

Piggott did make it to Newmarket, but only just. After six days he was still very weak and the heavy bandaging he now wore inside a specially prepared helmet gave him an almost freakish look. What other jockey would have made it at all? And what owner allowed him to ride? Certainly not Roberto's John Galbreath! But Lester was to confound everyone for the umpteenth time and bring home classic winner number twenty-four in a desperately close finish.

Fairy Footsteps had stamina, so Lester decided to 'wait in front' applying just an ounce or two more pressure whenever he sensed a challenge unwinding behind him. The tactics worked brilliantly, and although six horses came at him in the final furlong, Lester just kept getting that little bit more out of his filly so that she passed the post a neck ahead of Eddie Hide on Tolmi and a further neck in front of Greville Starkey on Go Leasing.

The roar of approval from the crowd was stupendous and as Lester led the filly back to the winner's enclosure his almost sheepish smile seemed to have echoes of the day at Epsom, almost ten years earlier, when he had led Roberto home through a thick wall of silence. Perhaps I am being too fanciful, but the afternoon was so laced with irony: Lester's appalling injury had made him the underdog and, as I have suggested, underdog translates as 'hero' to the British.

Of course, it wasn't long before Lester was back in the news for controversial reasons. Once again he had been chosen to displace a stable jockey on a fancied classic ride, this time the veteran Irishman Wally Swinburn on Blue Wind, the Oaks favourite. Swinburn is the father of Walter Swinburn, the brilliant youngster who partnered Shergar to all his great triumphs and later, on All Along, landed nearly one million dollars in races in France and America. After Walter's runaway twelve-length Derby win on Shergar, the press, at least, was praying for a family double with Wally in the Oaks.

Blue Wind's Irish trainer Dermot Weld had no trouble dismissing Fleet Street's suggestion. Since Fairy Footsteps had proved short of her best since Newmarket, Cecil did not even enter her for Epsom and that left Lester once more available. Weld had never won a classic. He knew he had this one in the palm of his hand – he wanted the best jockey.

Weld's confidence was justified. Blue Wind proved an outstanding filly and Lester was able to ride her pretty much as he liked. In the early stages he lay back and let Leap Lively set the furious pace, but then, shortly after entering the straight, he shot Blue Wind to the front before anyone else had gathered their mounts for the final-furlong flourish. And Blue Wind just kept on going, finally crossing the line a massive seven lengths clear of Madam Gay with Leap Lively staying on to be third, a further ten lengths back. I doubt if Lester has ever won a classic more easily, unless it was his 1983 Derby winner, Teenoso.

'When I let him go it was all over in a matter of strides,' Lester told the waiting press that day as they stood outside the Epsom weighing room waiting for further pearls to drop. With this, his ninth Derby behind him, Lester was in an unusually talkative mood and despite the ease of Teenoso's victory was quick to admit, 'This was not one of the best Derbies'. But never mind, it was the win that counted as the whole nation became involved in the race to beat Frank Buckle's record.

Almost inevitably, the Teenoso ride had been dropped straight into Lester's lap. Steve Cauthen had won twice on the colt in his two trial outings, but because he was claimed by his stable to ride The Noble Player in the Derby, it was left to Lester to choose between Teenoso, Tolomeo and Wassl. It was the sudden change in the ground that persuaded him to go for Geoffrey Wragg's mount, a horse that was in its element in soft ground. That was one time Lester chose brilliantly, but a few months later, his judgement was expensively wrong.

The Parisian art dealer Daniel Wildenstein had in All Along an animal of exceptional ability and both he and trainer Bianconne had high hopes for it in the Arc. Lester was booked early on, and as the weeping summer which had brought out the best in Teenoso suddenly changed to blistering warmth, Lester looked to be on another good bet. Then, in September, the rains returned and the jockey began to have his doubts. Longchamp in October . . . bound to be a bit soft, isn't it? The one factor that was known about All Along was that really soft ground torpedoed him, so when Lester was also offered the ride on Awasad, a known soft-ground performer, he changed course.

Richard Baerlein considers that particular sleight of hand was pushing luck to the ultimate extreme. Wildenstein was known to be a very strong-minded character, not one to suffer duplicity – perceived or otherwise – with any degree of lightness. When Lester announced that he would ride Awasad the Frenchman immediately responded with, 'That man will never ride for me again.' It is not an unfamiliar theme, but in racing it frequently has a hollow ring. Not this time. Wildenstein kept his word and, in doing so, created an almost nightmarish problem for his English trainer Henry Cecil who was forced to juggle his strong Wildenstein string between other top jockeys.

'When it comes down to it, Lester was just a bad judge of the weather in 1983, and that was his hard luck,' says Baerlein. 'If it had been this year [1984] he would have got away with it, but he decided the ground for the Arc is always heavy and as All Along can't go in the deep, why should he be bothered riding All Along? He'd already agreed to do it, so he was at fault, but he really did back a very heavy loser there. I know Swinburn got about $500,000 for winning in America and it probably cost Lester a million dollars, the whole package. That must have hurt more than anything.'

All Along, of course, not only won the Arc with ease but also the Washington International. The Wildenstein–Piggott split was to break up, or at least make unworkable to any practical degree, the partnership with his old friend Henry Cecil.

It was one thing to miss out on all that lovely money, it was quite another to be told by Wildenstein that he would never ride his horses again. This decision was in a slightly different league from the celebrated lambasting Lester received from Lambourn trainer Ben Leigh after his handling of a particular stable fancy. Leigh was usually going some if he hit double figures in a season. 'Have a heart guv, you'll bankrupt me!' protested Lester in mock horror when the trainer pronounced his weighty verdict.

What now complicated life for Piggott was that he was retained as stable jockey for champion trainer Cecil, a close friend as well as employer. Cecil had around thirty Wildenstein horses in his yard, many in the top bracket, and he didn't want to lose them. He didn't want to lose Lester either, and for a while Cecil seemed about to embark on the Roman solution and impale himself on his own sword. 'I felt that unless I could establish continuity with a stable jockey acceptable to all my owners, I should pack up. There was no more fun in training, I just felt like packing it all in.'

Whether Cecil would have stuck to his guns is arguable, but I think he would. For all his skill and brilliant eye for detail and planning, he has never lost the notion that horse-racing is fun. It *is* a business, but it is still fun. He is also quite a sentimental man and his friendship with Lester goes back a very long way. Lester and Susan Piggott were guests when Henry Cecil married Julie Murless; Lester even wrote the foreword to Cecil's amusing autobiography *On the Level* in which Piggott noted, 'I have never been happier than in my present job as first jockey to Warren Place. Henry and I look forward to many more years of success together before we are turned out to grass.'

So there was no question of Piggott being fired. Cecil could never bring himself to that, so Lester showed far more sensitivity in the matter than he is normally given credit for. He agreed that it would be better if he left the stable and returned to a freelance career in 1985. In making that decision he was effectively signalling retirement. There was clearly no way he was going back out into the cold again.

Lester and Henry Cecil reached agreement in a forty-five-minute meeting on the gallops at Newmarket and then, with exquisite timing, announced the decision on the eve of the 1984 Derby. It practically swept everything else off the sports pages. 'We were both moist eyed and far from happy when we made the decision to break,' Cecil told the press. 'It was not possible to retain two top class jockeys with Lester and Mr Wildenstein still at loggerheads and, as Lester only wanted another year, we decided it was better if we broke. But we are the best of friends and Lester has promised that if I need him at any of the meetings I am covering next year, he will be pleased to ride for me.'

Lester seemed philosophical about it all: 'It was bound to happen after the disagreement between me and the stable's main owner, Daniel Wildenstein. He said he wouldn't have me on his horses and that virtually split the yard in half as far as I was concerned. I'm sorry about it but it was inevitable. The situation couldn't have been allowed to continue.'

For Cecil, at least the blow was cushioned by the signing of American Steve Cauthen from the Barry Hills stable. Cauthen had been with the Lambourn trainer ever since coming to England from America in 1979 and losing him was a bitter blow. Said Hills: 'I'm terribly disappointed he's leaving me. He is a great jockey and at the moment I have no plans to replace him.' Hills has retained that dignified and diplomatic posture ever since while others have gone in to bat on his behalf on the question of loyalty. Cauthen, the argument runs, owes his success to his trainer; therefore, he should stay put. It is a curious position for anyone to hold, although emotions do tend to run high in racing circles when the jockey seesaw begins. Pat Eddery was accused of disloyalty when he left Peter Walwyn's stables to replace Lester Piggott with Vincent O'Brien. It was the obvious move for a young man of talent and ambition, but the moral pressure on Eddery was even greater because it was Walwyn's earlier vigorous defence of his jockey's riding of a Daniel Wildenstein horse that led to Wildenstein removing all his horses from Walwyn's yard.

So trainers play for high stakes when they oppose wealthy and powerful owners and jockeys do owe a degree of loyalty to the men who support them. But in the case of Eddery, the jockey had remained with Walwyn for some time afterwards and even when the 'offer he couldn't refuse' came along, old-fashioned loyalty nearly made him turn it down. So I must absolve Eddery and one must absolve Cauthen too. Ambition was always going to demand that one day he would reach out and exploit the full measure of his talent.

As for Lester, the ultimate pragmatist, a debate on loyalty would probably provoke a giant yawn. For him, loyalty is a personal conception: loyalty is to one's self, especially in a game like racing. It was interesting to hear his account of the Wildenstein split, a split, incidentally, that was precipitated long before the Arc when Lester rode the Frenchman's classy Vacarme at Goodwood in the Richmond Stakes. Lester's horse was so superior to the field that he knew he could win the race in any way he liked. That he chose to do so like some burrowing animal wriggling through the field brought down the full wrath of stewardship on his head. He was stood down and Vacarme relegated to last place. Guy Wildenstein, speaking on behalf of his father, asked open-mouthed: 'Does this Lester like giving owners heart attacks?'

A few months later, Papa Wildenstein himself was declaring apoplectically, 'That man will never ride for me again!' when Lester decided to 'stick by an earlier booking for John Dunlop'.

'I don't know what all the fuss was about,' said Lester. 'Mr Wildenstein took it badly but this kind of thing happens every day in racing. It's a bit like the old three card trick –

you pick the wrong one occasionally. All Along's French trainer was under the mistaken impression I had definitely accepted the ride, but it was a case of wires being crossed.'

There was no confusion over Lester's ride in the 1984 Derby. In a bloodless coup, he inherited the ride from Guy Harwood's stable jockey, Greville Starkey, after an unpleasant shoulder injury had been slow to heal. It made a nice change for Lester to get a full endorsement from the man he had replaced, but Starkey was not only happy to stand down, he was convinced that Alphabatim would give Lester that much-coveted tenth Derby. So were a lot of punters who suddenly brought a dead market back to life after the race had practically been conceded to Vincent O'Brien's wonder colt, El Gran Senor.

The galvanizing effect Piggott can have on a betting market was illustrated by the fact that over 25 million pounds was gambled on the Derby when the best earlier projections had been barely 16 million. 'It must be down to that old Piggott magic,' said a happy Ladbroke's spokesman. El Gran Senor didn't win the Derby, nor did Lester. Instead it was Vincent O'Brien's son David who landed his first classic with the splendidly ridden Secreto. There wasn't much in it. Just enough for the bookmakers to change their holiday flights from Barbados to the Isle of Wight. But the coming of David signalled a new era which promises great excitement for the future, especially with that good old Northern Dancer blood still sploshing around all over the place. When Vincent O'Brien explored that strain, he really *did* uncover racing's equivalent of the philosopher's stone.

I doubt if Lester was any more disappointed than he ever is when a Derby doesn't go his way, because, for all his trumpeting of the claims of Alphabatim, it was really El Gran Senor that had caught his imagination that year. In his *Daily Star* column, he had written: 'He certainly looks the business and hasn't put a foot wrong so far. If he stays, it's all over.' He also noted with some perception: 'Secreto is the dark horse of the race.' So there was no tenth Derby to celebrate. That would have to remain a pleasure deferred. But over the hill another target beckoned – the Oaks.

This. time there was no super horse in sight. By general consent, the fillies of 1984 were an average bunch with Optimistic Lass, Malaak and Circus Plume perhaps the chief fancies. Lester had ridden Circus Plume for the first time at Newbury three weeks before the big race. He had been quite impressed by her temperament and willingness to battle on under pressure. She also had a useful turn of foot and with the ground certain to be hard and fast the arithmetic seemed about right. Circus Plume's trainer John Dunlop was happy enough to give him the ride, although Willie Carson, who normally takes the Dunlop top fancies when not engaged by Dick Hern, was equally keen to get aboard.

In a sense, it proved to be one of the great Oaks of recent years, as exciting as it was unpredictable. Malaak, with Willie Shoemaker imported expensively from America, looked a sound investment for trainer Michael Stoute when she hit the front early in the straight but then, mysteriously, she ran out of puff leaving Circus Plume, Optimistic Lass, Poquito Queen and the 66/1 outsider, Media Luna, to dispute the finish. Lester held back Circus Plume until the final furlong, but no sooner had she got her nose in front than Media Luna swept her back again. Trainer Paul Kellaway seemed set to land a remarkable gamble and Paul Cook rode the filly for all he was worth in the last furlong.

But they had reckoned without Lester's all-consuming hunger for that twenty-seventh classic, and with the game Circus Plume responding to the driving force on her back, the Dunlop combination gradually reeled Media Luna back in again. Ten yards from the post Circus Plume stuck out her neck and held the margin as they crossed the line. It was thrilling stuff and Lester's supporters made sure their man knew just how much they appreciated his brilliance as the winner's enclosure became a sea of celebration. Just one classic target left.

Now it was 15 September and the hot, dry summer of 1984 sprang a sudden leak. A mushy-grey sky hung like a clammy veil over the famous Doncaster racecourse as thousands of racegoers streamed through the turnstiles on their way to a coronation. For this was St Leger Day, the day when Lester

Keith Piggott, OBE, would be officially acclaimed as the greatest jockey the world had ever seen. Just one more classic victory would take him beyond Buckle, and with the comforting thought of the favourite, Commanche Run, beneath him, he seemed certain to achieve it.

He had already achieved a great deal simply by securing the ride. By rights (moral, not legal) Commanche Run should have been partnered by the American Darrel McHargue, stable jockey to Newmarket trainer Luca Cumani, but in the week preceding the race, the horse's owner, Ivan Allan, had intervened and installed Piggott instead. It was no great surprise. Allan and Piggott were long-standing friends and 'jocking-off' other riders in favour of the eleven-times champion jockey had become the norm, not the exception, when the big prizes were at stake. Cumani had fought hard for his man to stay on board but there was no escaping the owner's logic – Lester was, and is, the best.

So McHargue dusted off his tennis racket and declared his intention of spending Saturday on the courts rather than the course. The controversy left Piggott totally unmoved. He had been down this road many times before and always he had kept his own counsel while the war of words raged all around him. But as one who had always been quick to see the humour in a situation, this particular incident provided him with an irresistible chance to add to the fund of famous Piggott one-liners.

As Piggott and his chauffeur sped north to Doncaster, the weather forecast came over on the car radio. 'It's raining hard, it's raining hard,' yelled the chauffeur to his passenger in the back seat. 'Hmm,' mused Lester, 'that's a shame.' And then with a chuckle, 'It might spoil McHargue's game of tennis. . .'

Ironically enough, his own chance of making history was at that moment hanging by the slenderest of threads. On the Wednesday before the weather turned spiteful, Commanche Run had stumbled on his way out to the gallops. 'There was blood on one knee and a graze on the other,' said his worried trainer. 'But I couldn't afford to miss the work so we hosed his legs for 15 minutes and then did the two canters we had planned.' Then they waited. This was brinkmanship on the grand scale; any swelling or infection would immediately rule the animal out. So owner, trainer, jockey and the millions of punters whose money would be riding on Piggott sweated it out until, on the morning of the big race, a nervous Cumani announced – 'The horse will run.'

So the last piece of the jigsaw that had been thirty years in the making was at last in Piggott's hands. Now, could he make it fit?

Among those opposing him would be the jockey everyone in racing acknowledged as his natural successor, the American Steve Cauthen. Already Cauthen was champion jockey-elect. At age sixteen he had blitzed his way to the US Triple Crown and a cool six million dollars in prize money. To everyone he was The Kid, the most revered sportsman in America, and later, when the apples turned sour, the most reviled. All jockeys suffer a slump, but Cauthen's was monumental. He couldn't buy his way onto a fancied racehorse, but just at the moment when his career hit rock bottom he was hauled from the gutter by the leading jockey's agent Lenny Goodman to replace the retiring Barulio Baeza. Cauthen was back, not quite with the glorious impact of 1977 but enough for his talent to flower once again.

In 1979, the owner/breeder Robert Sangster, who in concert with Vincent O'Brien had practically annexed the European classics, startled the racing world by importing Cauthen to England. He joined the Lambourn stables of Barry Hills and his impact was immediate as Tap on Wood won the 2,000 Guineas. Two seasons of consolidation followed as he 'learned his trade' all over again, but by 1982 he had shown that he had mastered the intricacies of English courses by topping 100 winners for the first time. Now he too stood on the threshold of history, and his mount, Baynoun, was a warmly fancied second favourite.

The drama that had punctuated Commanche Run's progress to Doncaster continued right up until the off. The colt sweated up for the first time in his racing career, perhaps infected by the tension of the occasion as the crowds swirled around him in the paddock. But there was no trouble at the start as they broke evenly and Guy Harwood's pacemaker Librate led them round the long sweeping turn. Lester tucked Commanche Run in behind the leader with Cauthen and Baynoun tracking him, and that is how they remained until the home straight when Commanche Run hit the front with Crazy, Shernazer, Baynoun and Alphabatim in hot pursuit. Now the moment of truth had arrived.

Lester pressed the accelerator still harder and suddenly he had only Cauthen for company as the American made a determined challenge. A furlong from home, it looked decisive. But somehow, Lester conjured just a little bit more from Commanche Run and that gamest of colts just kept his nose in front all the way to the line. Doncaster was suddenly a madhouse. Even the imperturbable Piggott was forced to smile as the huge crowd practically swept him into the winner's enclosure. 'I didn't realize they cared so much,' said the bemused jockey as the human tide swirled around him. Afterwards he would reveal just how slender the margin had been as he admitted, 'A furlong out I thought I would be beaten. But Commanche Run is very game and he knew what was needed.'

What *we* needed was champagne. Lots of it, and the celebrations continued long into the night as pundits and punters, sages and sightseers, joined forces in toasting a giant slice of sporting history. Of course it would have been appropriate if Lester had announced his retirement then and there, but, fuelled with the kind of high-octane charge that only he understands, he announced instead, 'I don't mean that to be my last classic.' After that there wasn't a dry eye in the house.

So the reporters and feature writers were happy to put away their notebooks for a little longer while the racing world was left to bite on the implications of another season with Piggott on the loose. And perhaps to reflect on some of the qualities and contradictions of the man who commands so much loyalty and affection and yet has offered nothing in return – except winners, of course. But sometimes it is all too easy to dismiss the deeper fires that lie banked within a performer on a public stage. Piggott of the grave countenance and monosyllabic speech is often misunderstood.

There is, for example, a mischievous vein of humour that runs throughout Lester's career. It isn't always appreciated, of course, especially if the butt of the joke is made to look a fool, which is what happened to French jockey Alain Lequeux at a meeting in Deauville.

Lester was riding African Hope, a lazy horse that needed to be constantly shown the whip. Unfortunately, at a crucial point in the race, Lester dropped his whip and was suddenly like a ship without a rudder. Quickly summing up the situation he pushed African Hope along until they were upsides of the leader, Lequeux. As the two animals moved in rhythm together Lequeux's whip came up. In a flash, Lester had snatched it away and driven African Hope pell-mell for the line.

The crowd went wild. So did the stewards, of course. Gallic humour did not stretch to such racecourse antics and Lester was stood down for twenty-one days, a suspension which caused him to miss the St Leger – won by Lequeux!

After the Deauville race, Willie Carson, still shaking his head in disbelief, asked Lester just what he thought he'd been up to.

'Well, I asked him for it,' replied the jockey.

'You what?' said Carson. 'You asked him for it? You can't speak French.'

'I said, "Le baton, s'il vous plait,"' came the deadpan reply.

Willie Carson knows Lester as well as anyone on the circuit and while their rivalry doesn't have quite the passionate intensity of the Piggott–Breasley or Piggott–Lewis battles of the sixties and seventies, it has its more vivid moments. Like at Ascot in 1984 when Carson brandished his whip at Piggott shortly after being pipped on the post in a fierce finish. As they crossed the line, Lester leaned across: 'I've stuffed you again,' he said. Willie was not amused. The course stewards who overheard the remark summoned both jockeys for an explanation.

'The video showed Carson flipping his whip at Piggott as they crossed the line,' said an official later. 'He was told not to do it again. Both jockeys dismissed the incident as "just a joke" although Carson later admitted, "I suppose Lester was a bit chuffed because he usually rides Popsi's Joy [Carson's mount]. But it was just a bit of fun and we are the best of mates.'"

Scobie Breasley used to say much the same thing through gritted teeth as he and Lester fought tooth and nail for the title in the early sixties. The Australian jockey Edgar Britt reveals how on one occasion at Sandown Park he seemed set to become the meat in a deadly sandwich as Lester and Scobie revved up like grand prix drivers at the start, each determined to beat the other to the inside rail. 'Hey, do your feuding when I'm not around,' he admonished the pair.

Christopher Poole, Breasley's biographer and one of the most entertaining racing writers, believes the feud was media-inspired and greatly exaggerated. In his book, *Scobie, a Lifetime in Racing*, he writes: 'The long drawn-out title race was good copy made even more sensational by the implication that Breasley and Piggott were at daggers drawn. They were not. But it is true to say that they were not bosom pals either.' Scobie's summary is simple: 'I didn't spend much time talking about Lester in those days and I doubt if he was very keen to talk about me.'

Battle lines were in fact drawn as early as 1960 when, according to Breasley, Piggott cut him up so badly in that race at Wolverhampton when he was almost forced over the rails. The Australian then deprived Lester of a big race win on the wonder filly Petite Etoile, trapping him in a pocket on the rails until his chance had gone. There was no repeat of the Wolverhampton incident, claims Breasley, and neither were there any recriminations from Lester.

Ground rules having now been established, both men concentrated on their singular pursuit of the champion's crown. Having worn it for the first time in 1960, Lester rather liked the feel of it and it was a crushing disappointment to lose out in 1961 when a fall, two days before the end of the season, virtually handed the title to Breasley. With his rival out of the saddle, Scobie managed to turn a precarious lead of four into an unassailable seven by riding a treble at Lingfield Park.

The intensity of the struggle made a deep impression on the sporting public. The contrasts between the fiery youngster and the calm middle-aged man were so marked that it was impossible to be neutral. You were either with Piggott or with Breasley: it was the Boat Race on horseback. In fact, the scenario didn't quite work out in 1962. Not for the first time, Lester was front-page news when it was found that he had 'made no effort to win' on Ione. The Jockey Club's six weeks ban meant that by the time Lester resumed riding, Scobie had practically lapped him. Fourth place with 96 winners was his worst total in four years.

Then in 1963, the public really got what it wanted. A neck-and-neck struggle all the way up the home stretch with the lead sometimes swapping twice daily when there was an evening programme being run. Fleet Street embraced this 'running story' with typical fervour and national newspapers carried the 'box score' on the front page of every edition. Few other sports stories have attracted such intense sustained coverage in this country, though in America a decade later, Hank Aaron's pursuit of Babe Ruth's home run record spilled well beyond the confines of baseball.

In the end, it was Breasley who triumphed again, and by the narrowest possible margin, 176 to 175. It was a crushing disappointment for Lester, a disappointment for once not cushioned by classic success and later laced with the kind of controversy that leaves a sour taste in the mouth for a long time afterwards.

As I say, Piggott and Breasley presented a contrast in both personality and style. Lester's all-action finish was thrilling to see, but it relied to perhaps an exaggerated degree on a flailing whip, which offended more than the purists. It didn't always go down too well with the public either, and after a race at Newbury, Lester was reported by a spectator to the RSPCA. The horse in question, Casabianca, was a talented but lazy animal; he needed firm as well as skilful handling. He got both that afternoon, though rather too much of the one as opposed to the other for the likes of Fleet Street. Once more the headlines screamed out Piggott's name.

The irony of the situation was that Casabianca was

trained at Warren Place by Noel Murless, perhaps the most sensitive trainer the sport has seen. He would rather lose a race than allow a horse to suffer and was sometimes criticized during his brilliant career for withdrawing animals he didn't think were 'quite right'. In some cases these were carrying a ton of punters' gold – Crepello in 1957 is a notable example – but his attitude never wavered. When confronted with the Casabianca allegations, he gave the public a much-needed definition of terms.

'Piggott gave the horse a smack on the hindquarters, where it doesn't hurt and it started forward more in surprise than anything else. That was all. There are jockeys who know how to hurt a horse – under the girth, across the belly – and will do so. But not Piggott. He may wave the whip a lot and certainly he is a determined rider. But cruel – never.'

The Casabianca incident rumbled on for a few weeks but it never came to a prosecution, private or otherwise, and was eventually stampeded into the background by the accelerating Piggott–Breasley battle. There was, incidentally, an interesting sequel, when Casabianca won the 1965 Royal Hunt Cup in one of the most celebrated finishes ever seen at Ascot. Once again Lester was forced to drive the animal every inch of the way home as Weepers Boy, Zaleucs, Blazing Scent, Balustrade and Old Tom all battled for the line. Somehow Lester got up to win by a head on the line, and when Casabianca returned to the stables there wasn't a mark on him.

It would be wrong to suggest that the Casabianca affair was an isolated incident. There were numerous occasions when Piggott's use of the whip drew censure, both official and unofficial. But I don't think that anyone in racing would ever describe him as 'cruel'. What is clearly endemic to his make-up, and an essential clue to his genius, is his determination to master everything. To master the horse, to master his body, to master his rivals. . . Being second at anything hurts and sometimes he seems prepared to make his own rules.

By 1964, Scobie Breasley was fifty and Lester had regained his crown. He was to hold it for the next eight years, but against no less determined a challenger than the Australian had been. This time the rival would be Geoff Lewis, the chirpy Welsh-born wizard who had taken up racing after reading of Lester's exploits as a boy – a bell boy, to be precise, at London's Savoy Hotel where both ends of the racing spectrum were represented. The penthouse suites housed owners, but the real punters were below stairs!

Lewis was a good jockey who never quite received his proper due. He was lucky to be around when they were handing out rides on such sensational animals as Mill Reef and Brigadier Gerard, animals whose exploits illuminated the post-Nijinsky seventies. Lewis and Mill Reef never let each other down, but because the colt was so outstanding, Lewis was never given full credit for his riding of it. As for the jockey's title, twice he seemed to have it within his grasp only for Lester to spring out of a trapdoor on the finishing line and snatch it away.

After taking so long to master Breasley, there was no way in which Lester was going to relinquish his crown. His was now a go-anywhere, ride-anything philosophy. Henry Cecil, the brilliant Newmarket trainer with whom Piggott won champion jockey titles in 1981 and 1982, tells in his autobiography of a typical Piggott ploy when Cecil was still perhaps a little green as a fully fledged guv'nor.

'Lewis looked like establishing a useful advantage from four booked rides at Hamilton Park, two of them on our horses. Two days before the meeting, Lester phoned to say, "I'll ride your two at Hamilton. Geoff will be at Nottingham."

'Seeing from the press that Lester was down to ride both my runners, Geoff rang up in a somewhat bemused state to ask what had happened. "Lester said you would be at Nottingham," I told him. "But that's a bloody jumping meeting!" exploded Geoff.' Needless to say, Lester won on Cecil's two plus two others for a four-timer that catapulted him ahead of his rival, and eventually to the title by 163 to 146.

Later, Piggott would lose interest in the title for its own sake, partly because he felt he had nothing left to prove but mainly because he had developed a consuming passion for the big races – and not just the classics. There was plenty of gold to be mined on the Continent and even further afield, America, Australia, the Far East. Such globe-trotting turned the championship mathematics around in favour of rising stars like Carson and Pat Eddery.

But they turned Lester's bank account around too. Part of the reason for the celebrated split with Noel Murless in 1966 and the decision to ride freelance the following year was that the champion had begun to realize his own worth. Richard Baerlein explained it to me this way:

> Murless's owners were basically the old type of owner-breeder who did everything by the book and they didn't give the extra presents which the modern man was coming along and giving. They were often very mean because the English aristocracy is notoriously mean and they didn't understand that you've got to give these guys extra encouragement because there are all sorts of bookmakers and others willing to give them God knows what to lose, so you've got to make it a bit better than the standard 10 per cent.
>
> In the sixties, the whole thing was turning into a business. I mean, there was dear old Gordon Richards who retired after being the greatest jockey there had ever been and he retired with very little money. The modern man is determined to end up rich if he's at the top of his profession and I think Lester always saw that. I think he decided that he wasn't going to be left out. Also, he wanted to go down in the record books as having ridden more classic winners than anyone else, and 10 Derby's, well that would be the ultimate. . .

The retirement stories have been around almost as long as Lester himself. In 1954, after suffering that notorious suspension, he was forced to shed so much weight in getting back to the saddle that many serious critics were ready to write him off there and then. A career under National Hunt rules seemed the logical alternative. Lester, of course, confounded his critics by beginning one of the most sustained and single-minded fasts in the history of sport. He beat his body into submission. Gone were the beloved ice cream, the steaks, the vegetables . . . in came black coffee, dry toast and perhaps a sliver or two of chicken. Later, the Churchillian cigar was enlisted to quell hunger pangs, and later still, the famous half-bottle of champagne.

The result of all this was a body so bereft of flesh that the muscles stood out like whipcords. The face became shrunken and hollow and as grey as the sheet that wasn't washed in Persil. 'He has a face like a well kept grave,' wrote one journalist in the *Observer*, and the description has never been bettered.

Not many jockeys survive the purgatory of constant deprivation. Scots ace Duncan Keith and TV's Jimmy Lindley are two notable casualties in recent times. Both gave up the unequal struggle when their very lives seemed suddenly to be at risk. In an earlier generation, Fred Archer, the jockey with whom Piggott is most often compared, became so depressed by it all that he blew his brains out during a bout of fever. He was twenty-nine and is still regarded by many historians as the greatest jockey of them all.

But Lester won his battle. The will was indomitable, the body finally obeyed and so today as he approaches fifty, he is able to eat as normally as anyone. Daughter Maureen says: 'He munches Yorkie bars all day long. This image of him living off champagne and cigars is nonsense today.'

But not in 1970. There was nothing normal about the Piggott regimen then, and at one point during that Nijinsky-dominated season he actually collapsed on the racecourse from the combined effects of exhaustion and starvation. In November he confided to the British press in Washington, before the running of the International, that he was totally and utterly exhausted. A spate of 'will he won't he?' retirement articles immediately followed and a chilling article in which a Dublin specialist who had made a close study of jockeys' problems declared: 'They spend half their lives walking from the sauna-bath to the toilet. Some of them leave the racecourse suffering from complete exhaustion with spasms in their hands and feet.'

Lester's reaction to all this was to cancel riding plans for the winter in Hong Kong and Australia and instead to rest in the warm sun of the Caribbean. The cure worked perfectly.

He returned full of vigour and renewed enthusiasm for the 1971 season. Never again would he step so close to the edge of the precipice.

Today, Lester keeps fit with working holidays, but in any case he no longer finds getting ready to ride much of a trial. 'The strange thing,' he wrote recently, 'is that instead of it becoming harder to get fit for a new season as I've grown older, it's got easier. In my younger days I was inclined to get much heavier during the winter, and it would be one hell of a shock to the system to get it off before the start of the flat, sweating, saunas, running. I reckon my body has been educated over the years and now knows the form. If I had to go back to taking off a lot of weight all of a sudden, I wouldn't be able to manage it.'

What Lester was admitting, of course, is that the only defence against spreading middle age is the treadmill. Step off it for a moment and you're finished. No wonder the celebrated retirement decision was left to gather dust on a high shelf. Until, that is, one of Lester's closest friends, Peter O'Sullevan, just happened to slip it into his own retirement column in the *Daily Express* 1985. It did not go unnoticed!

I have a sneaking suspicion that Lester had anticipated the explosion that would follow. He was halfway across the Atlantic with his wife Susan when the follow-ups appeared in other papers and pundits were wheeled into television studios to pay their tributes. So who could confirm it? Certainly not youngest daughter Tracy who fielded reporters' questions at the Newmarket home with a bland, 'It's the first I've heard of it.' Owner Charles St George, a close friend of Piggott's and one of his leading patrons, also played dumb. 'He's never mentioned retirement to me,' he declared. But the person who really felt the full force of the blast was Lester's business manager, the New Zealand-born Mike Watt. He tiptoed around a statement that said in part, 'While the decision to retire in the foreseeable future is confirmed no firm date has been fixed.' Was he really caught flat-footed? It would seem so. And was it one of Lester's practical jokes to have Fleet Street running around chasing its own tail?

If it was, the joke was not appreciated at the offices of the

Daily Star where Lester's expensively ghosted column is one of the paper's biggest features. 'PIGGOTT FURY – I AM NOT GOING YET', screamed the headline of the morning of 22 January, but the story did not match that strident tone. 'Speaking from their executive suite in a Pasadena hotel', declared the paper, 'Susan Piggott has issued a statement to the *Daily Star* on Lester's behalf. She said: "What's all the fuss about? He will retire one day, of course, but he hasn't told me and I should know. We have just arrived from a long, gruelling flight and Lester wants his rest. We don't know what they are saying over there in Britain, and frankly, we don't care. Lester will retire when he is good and ready."'

That lack of a denial, despite the headline, seemed to clinch it. It surprised no one in racing, not even the *Daily Star* racing desk. What caught them on the hop was the timing of the newsbreak, and that, of course, was pure Piggott.

So, now we are left with the 64,000 dollar question. What kind of a trainer will Lester make?

'Strictly on the form book the odds are against him,' says Brough Scott. 'Of all the top jockeys who have switched this century, only Harry Wragg has succeeded to the same level as a trainer.' Scott also points out that Piggott has already dipped his toe into the water with a seventy-strong string that ran last season under the banner of his former chauffeur, Michael Hinchcliffe. Seven winners was the sum total of their efforts. But perhaps it is unfair to cite that experiment. After all, Lester was a busy man last season chasing winners on the track so his involvement could only have been peripheral at best.

Perhaps, then, it is more relevant to heed the words of Doug Smith, himself a former champion jockey turned trainer who now runs a thriving bloodstock agency in Newmarket. 'In my opinion,' says Smith, 'he will approach training as he does riding, he will be totally dedicated. But he will find it a lot of hard work. The hardest part is the paperwork because there are so many restrictions nowadays. He'll love being out with his horses, seeing some of them work well and four or five days later seeing them winning just as you'd planned. But then he'll have to put up with the times when things

go wrong, when you see them looking as if they'll win a furlong out and then they go out like a light. That's the hardest
part.'

Smith, though, faced other problems as a trainer which
Lester is unlikely to encounter. As Hotspur of the *Daily Telegraph* pointed out in an article published shortly after the
'retirement announcement', Smith was forced to quit for
economic reasons. Money looks to be the least of Piggott's
problems. Not only does he own Eve Lodge stables in Hamilton Road – which since 1975 has been leased successively to
Bill Marshall, Michael Albina and Michael Hinchcliffe – but
he also owns two other well-appointed yards. Smith's owners
quite simply died off and the former champion jockey was
not the sort of character to go touting for new business. The
boxes stayed empty, the bills mounted. The break was
inevitable.

Piggott is unlikely to feel such inhibitions, and in any case
he should hardly need to. He has already been promised the
support of the powerful Maktoum family for his first crop of
yearlings, and he will inevitably receive similar support from
his friend Charles St George. Filling the 129-box yard with
quality horseflesh will not be the problem. How different
from the reaction Sir Gordon Richards is said to have
encountered when he approached Sir Victor Sassoon thirty
years previously. 'Why should I trust my animals to a begin-
ner?' replied the formidable Sir Victor to the man who had
twenty-two times been champion jockey.

Richard Baerlein concedes that Piggott will be bringing
formidable gifts to his new role. 'The one thing about Lester
is that he watches everything that goes on in a race. He
knows what every other horse is doing, so that afterwards he
can say, "right, I want to ride that next time out." He has
uncanny judgement. That's one of the things that lifts him
above all the others – as a jockey. But you just can't tell
whether he will be a wonderful trainer. There's an awful lot
of luck in it you know.

'As a judge of a horse's potential you'd have to say he has
everything in his favour, but that doesn't necessarily mean
he is going to be in the same class as a Vincent O'Brien

because he has spent so much time riding. National Hunt jockeys make much better trainers than flat jockeys because they are with their horses so much more and are forever studying their legs. The jockey sort of rides the animal schooling and then comes back to the stable and looks at what has happened. I think the National Hunt rider goes through a much better grounding than a flat race jockey who jumps on it, rides it, jumps on another one, probably has three or four in a morning – and then nips off to the races. So it is not a foregone conclusion that he will be a success.'

For his own part, Lester has never expressed any doubts. Once, when asked by a reporter how long it would take him to learn his new profession, he replied, 'About five minutes'. A joke. But was it a joke when, as Brough Scott reports, he turned to Charles St George and said, 'Of course I'll be a success. I'll be the best trainer you've ever seen.'

And how will we remember him – as the greatest ever?

Richard Baerlein: 'It's difficult, no, it's impossible. You really cannot compare one generation with another because the person who is there at the time is always the best. Gordon Richards won more races that he should have lost than anybody else but Lester wins races that Gordon could not have won, because of his style. Gordon was a bit set. Lester is absolutely fluid. On the other hand Lester does occasionally get beaten when he should have won by being too clever. I think the thing that will really stick in my mind will be his effort on Roberto in the Derby. Nobody else could have won that day.'

Perhaps the last word should be left with former Royal jockey Harry Carr: 'Piggott is the best that got on a horse, anywhere, anytime. . .'

Appendix:
Racing Career

Riding Record 1948-84

	1st	2nd	3rd	Unplaced	Mounts	Champion jockey position
1948	1	2	0	21	24	–
1949	6	8	10	96	120	–
1950	52	45	39	268	404	11th
1951	51	36	40	305	432	13th
1952	79	47	70	424	620	5th
1953	41	32	45	323	441	15th
1954	42	38	30	152	262	18th
1955	103	84	77	266	530	3rd
1956	129	79	75	359	642	3rd
1957	122	92	83	280	577	3rd
1958	83	81	64	309	537	6th
1959	142	96	85	236	559	3rd
1960	170	107	75	288	640	1st
1961	164	108	73	358	703	2nd
1962	96	77	50	235	458	4th
1963	175	109	71	302	657	2nd
1964	140	106	70	310	626	1st

	1st	2nd	3rd	Unplaced	Mount	Champion jockey position
1965	160	110	81	304	655	1st
1966	191	89	101	301	682	1st
1967	117	100	64	276	557	1st
1968	139	98	75	268	580	1st
1969	163	95	87	255	600	1st
1970	162	110	68	246	586	1st
1971	162	120	89	259	630	1st
1972	103	69	74	218	464	4th
1973	129	80	58	216	483	2nd
1974	143	91	73	279	586	2nd
1975	113	88	61	265	527	3rd
1976	87	68	51	196	402	7th
1977	103	82	62	265	512	4th
1978	97	78	61	249	485	5th
1979	77	54	40	232	403	6th
1980	156	96	65	318	635	2nd
1981	179	113	87	324	703	1st
1982	188	87	94	329	698	1st
1983	150	109	64	318	641	2nd
1984	100	79	72	240	491	–
1985	34	32	31	160	257	–
Totals	4349	2995	2415	10050	19809	

Piggott also rode in 56 hurdle races, winning 20 times

Derby Record

Year	Horse	Position	Odds
1951	Zucchero	unplaced	28/1
1952	Gay Time	2nd	25/1
1953	Prince Charlemagne	unplaced	66/1
1954	Never Say Die	1st	33/1
1955	Windsor Sun	unplaced	33/1
1956	Affiliation Order	unplaced	33/1
1957	Crepello	1st	6/4
1958	Boccaccio	unplaced	20/1
1959	Carnoustie	6th	10/1
1960	St Paddy	1st	7/1
1961	did not ride	–	–
1962	did not ride	–.	–
1963	Corpora	5th	100/8
1964	Sweet Moss	unplaced	100/8
1965	Meadow Court	2nd	10/1
1966	Right Noble	unplaced	9/2
1967	Ribocco	2nd	22/1
1968	Sir Ivor	1st	4/5
1969	Ribofilio	5th	7/2
1970	Nijinsky	1st	11/8
1971	The Parson	6th	16/1
1972	Roberto	1st	3/1
1973	Cavo Doro	2nd	12/1
1974	Arthurian	unplaced	28/1
1975	Bruni	unplaced	16/1
1976	Empery	1st	10/1
1977	The Minstrel	1st	5/1
1978	Inkerman	unplaced	4/1
1979	Milford	unplaced	15/2
1980	Monteverdi	unplaced	8/1
1981	Shotgun	4th	7/1
1982	did not ride	–	–
1983	Teenoso	1st	9/2
1984	Alphabatim	5th	11/2

Classic Winners

The Derby

Never Say Die	1954
Crepello	1957
St Paddy	1960
Sir Ivor	1968
Nijinsky	1970
Roberto	1972
Empery	1976
The Minstrel	1977
Teenoso	1983

St Leger

St Paddy	1960
Aurelius	1961
Ribocco	1967
Ribero	1968
Nijinsky	1970
Athens Wood	1971
Boucher	1972
Commanche Run	1984

2,000 Guineas

Crepello	1957
Sir Ivor	1968
Nijinsky	1970

1,000 Guineas

Humble Duty	1970
Fairy Footsteps	1981

The Oaks

Carrozza	1957
Petite Etoile	1959
Valoris	1966
Juliette Marny	1975
Blue Wind	1981
Circus Plume	1984

Bibliography

Among the many sources of reference consulted the following books proved especially valuable and are recommended to any readers who want to broaden their interest in racing in general and Lester Piggott in particular.

Baerlein, Richard, *Nijinsky: Triple Crown Winner*, Pelham, 1971

Bailey, Ivor N., *Lester Piggott, Champion Jockey*, Arthur Barker, 1972

Breasley, Scobie and Poole, Christopher, *Scobie: a lifetime in racing*, Queen Anne Press, 1984

Bromley, Peter, *The Price of Success: the authorized biography of Ryan Price*, Hutchinson, 1982

Cecil, Henry, *On the Level*, Harrap, 1983

Duval, Claude, *Lester*, Stanley Paul, 1972

　　　　　　　　Pat on the Back: the story of Pat Eddery, Stanley Paul, 1976

　　　　　　　　Willie Carson: a biography, Stanley Paul, 1980

Emery, David (ed), *Who's Who in Flat Racing*, Queen Anne Press, 1984

Fitzgeorge-Parker, Tim, *The Guv'nor: a biography of Sir Noel Murless*, Collins, 1980

Herbert, Ivor and O'Brien, Jacqueline, *Vincent O'Brien's Great Horses*, Pelham, 1984

Lawrence, John G.T. (John Oaksey), *The Story of Mill Reef*, Michael Joseph, 1974

Lawton, James, *Lester Piggott*, Arthur Barker, 1980

Mortimer, Roger, *The Flat: flat racing in Britain since 1939*, Allen and Unwin, 1979
    The History of the Derby Stakes, Michael Joseph, 1973

Onslow, Richard, *The Heath and the Turf: a history of Newmarket*, Arthur Barker, 1971

Payne, Ken, *The Coup*, Futura, 1978

Poole, Christopher, *Classic Treble: the Sangster-Piggott-O'Brien partnership*, Queen Anne Press, 1982

Scott, Brough, *On and Off the Rails*, Victor Gollancz, 1984

Scott, Brough and Cranham, Gerry, *The World of Flat Racing*, World's Work, 1983

Seth-Smith, Michael, *Knight of the Turf: the life and times of Sir Gordon Richards*, Hodder and Stoughton, 1980

Index

Races are listed under the name of the racecourse

MORE READING FROM NEL

SEBASTIAN COE WITH
DAVID MILLER
☐ 98857 6   Running Free   £1.50

RICHARD EVANS
☐ 05586 8   McEnroe: A Rage For Perfection   £2.50

CHRIS EVERT & NEIL ADMUR
☐ 05567 1   Chrissie   £1.60

COLIN TURNER
☐ 05783 6   In Search of Shergar (Illustrated)   £2.25

All these books are available at your local bookshop or newsagent, or can be ordered direct from the publisher. Just tick the titles you want and fill in the form below.

Prices and availability subject to change without notice.

CORONET BOOKS, P.O. Box 11, Falmouth, Cornwall.

Please send cheque or postal order, and allow the following for postage and packing:

U.K. – 55p for one book, plus 22p for the second book, and 14p for each additional book ordered up to a £1.75 maximum.

B.F.P.O. and EIRE – 55p for the first book, plus 22p for the second book, and 14p per copy for the next 7 books, 8p per book thereafter.

OTHER OVERSEAS CUSTOMERS – £1.00 for the first book, plus 25p per copy for each additional book.

Name ....

Address ....

....